COVER ART BY
ANTONIO FUSO
& EMILIO LECCE

COVER COLORS BY
JASON LEWIS

COLLECTION EDITS BY
JUSTIN EISINGER
AND ALONZO SIMON

COLLECTION DESIGN BY
JEFF POWELL

PUBLISHER
TED ADAMS

Facebook: **facebook.com/idwpublishing**
Twitter: **@idwpublishing**
YouTube: **youtube.com/idwpublishing**
Tumblr: **tumblr.idwpublishing.com**
Instagram: **instagram.com/idwpublishing**

ISBN: 978-1-63140-532-7   19 18 17 16   1 2 3 4

Originally published as DRIVE issues #1–4.

SPECIAL THANKS TO JAMES SALLIS AND THE POISONED PEN TEAM FOR THEIR INVALUABLE ASSISTANCE.

Library of Congress Cataloging-in-Publication Data

Names: Benedetto, Michael, author. | Fuso, Antonio, illustrator. | Lecce, Emilio, illustrator. | Lewis, Jason, illustrator. | Cvetkovic, Frank, illustrator. | Eisinger, Justin, editor. | Sallis, James, 1944- Drive.
Title: James Sallis' Drive / written by Michael Benedetto ; pencils by Antonio Fuso ; inks by Emilio Lecce ; colors by Jason Lewis ; letters and logo design by Frank Cvetkovic ; series edits by Justin Eisinger.
Other titles: Drive
Description: San Diego, CA : IDW Publishing, 2016. | "Originally published as DRIVE issues #1-4."
Identifiers: LCCN 2015049923 | ISBN 9781631405327 (pbk.)
Subjects: LCSH: Stunt performers--Comic books, strips, etc. | Stunt driving--Comic books, strips, etc. | Graphic novels. | Noir fiction. | Comic books, strips, etc.
Classification: LCC PN6727.B3785 J36 2016 | DDC 741.5/973--dc23
LC record available at http://lccn.loc.gov/2015049923

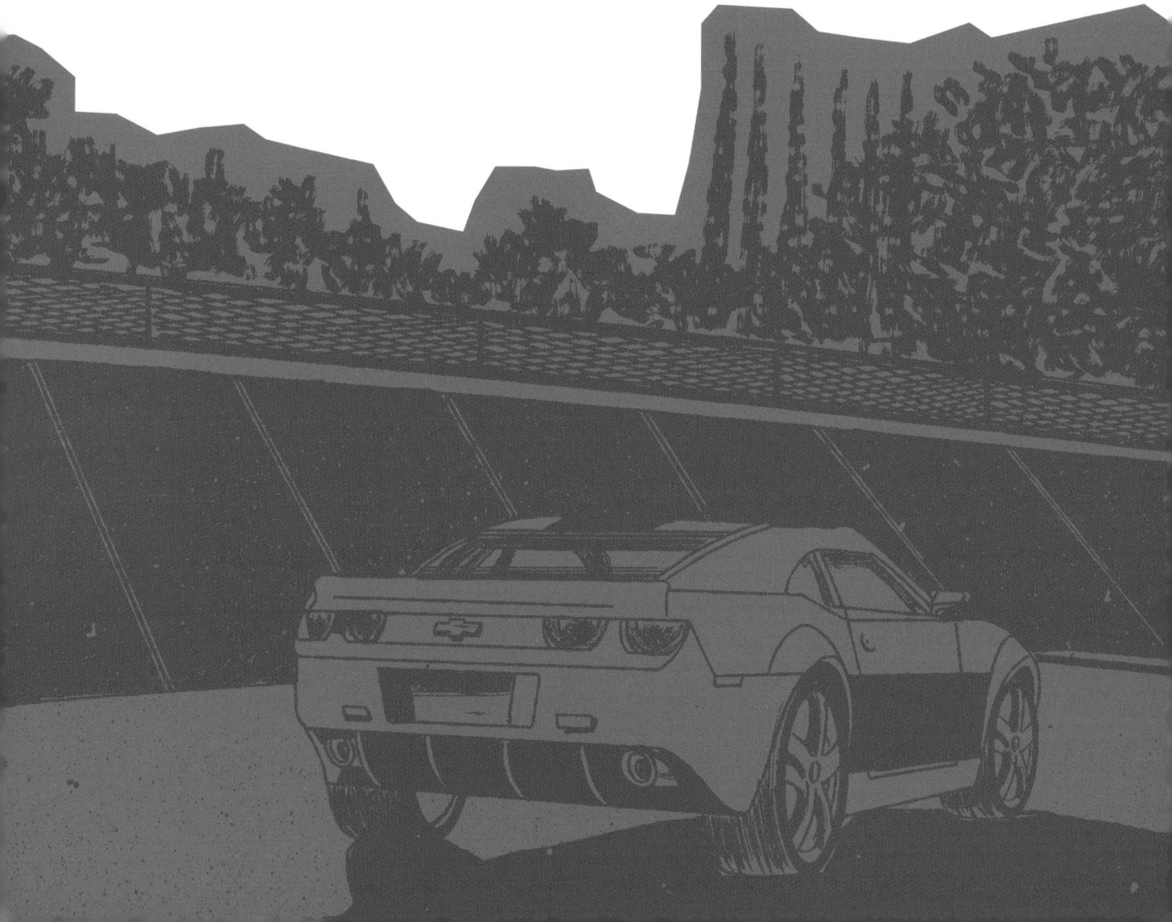

James Sallis'

DR1VE

WRITTEN BY
MICHAEL BENEDETTO

PENCILS BY
ANTONIO FUSO

INKS BY
EMILIO LECCE

COLORS BY
JASON LEWIS

LETTERS & LOGO DESIGN BY
FRANK CVETKOVIC

SERIES EDITS BY
JUSTIN EISINGER

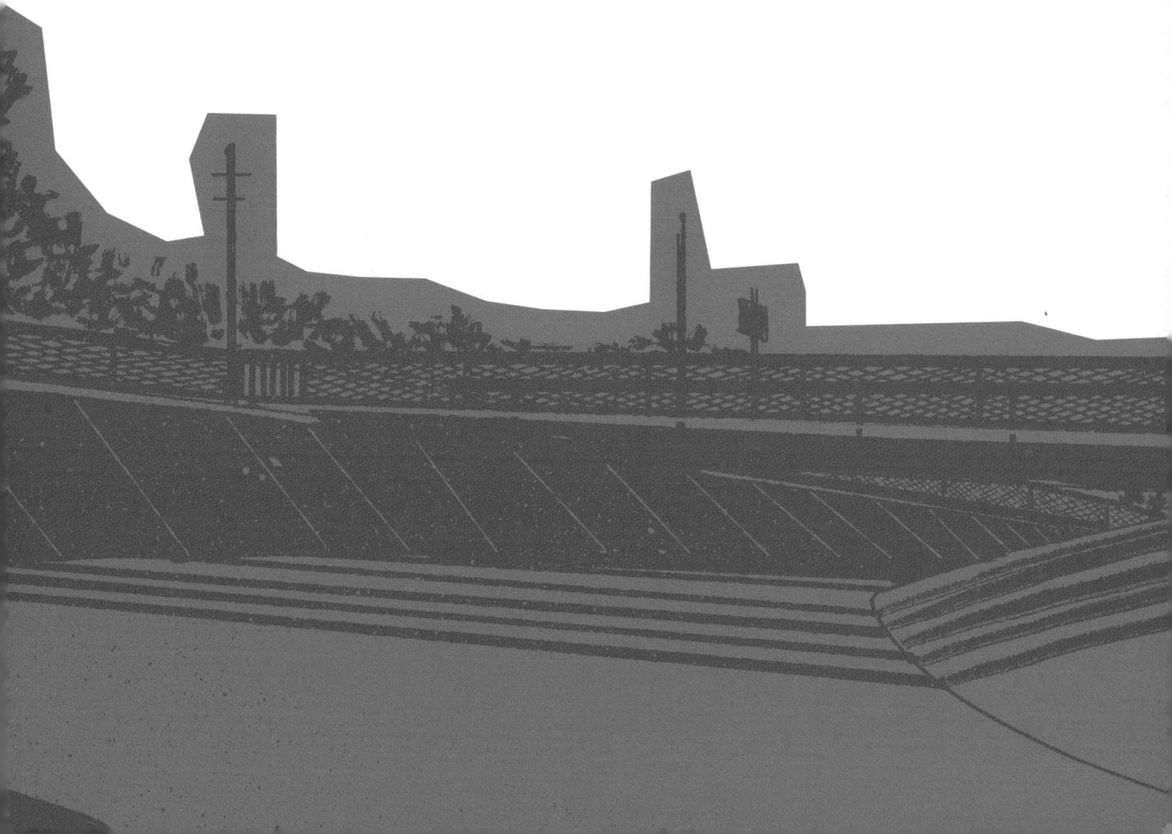

HOW I LEARNED TO DRIVE

BY JAMES SALLIS

For some time I'd had the idea to write a contemporary version of the paperback original, a novel that would capture the rattiness, energy, glowering doom and general unsavoriness of those wonderful old Gold Medal books, but with an updated attitude.

Half a page of notes scrawled on a legal pad in New Orleans, essentially the first page of this novel, had lain dormant and coiled in a file for years, following me from city to city.

Then, when Dennis McMillan asked me to contribute a new noir story to his anthology *Measures of Poison*, the thing started unwinding. Time, I figured, to take those notes out for a test drive. I pulled them out, did a bit of mouth to mouth, and wrote the story. The ride went well, so I figured I might as well invest in the car. If I was sufficiently intrigued by the character to want to know more, readers might be as well.

Written in a concentrated push during a time when I was housebound, the novel proved problematic. It was not the sort of thing publishers seem to be looking for these days. It looped back and forth in a kind of narrative free association and didn't spell much of anything out, trusting the reader to make connections.

And, in this time of doorstop, wrist-spraining, blockbuster novels, it was short. Very short. Pygmy short.

Not that I much cared. I had written the novel (as, earlier, I wrote *Death Will Have Your Eyes*) out of love for a particular mode of crime novel and in homage to favorite writers, as the dedication demonstrates:

> *To Ed McBain, Donald Westlake, and Larry Block*
> *—three great American writers*

Granted, I had in mind as well, a throng of others standing behind us: Jim Thompson, David Goodis, Horace McCoy, Richard Prather, Donald Hamilton, Philip Atlee. Muscular books, lean books—machines, really, that always got the job done. It was the *tone* I was after, the *feel* of these things, claustrophobic and driven, what Geoffrey O'Brien in his brilliant *Hardboiled America: The Lurid Years of Paperbacks* called a new urban poetry, trembling on the edge of the real.

Well, the pretty girls weren't going to dance with me. I knew that. My agent knew that. It was going to be a hard sell.

Short. Dark. Weird.

We figured we'd eventually publish it, it would like most books fall screaming off the edge of the world, and that would be that. I'd make a little money on foreign sales. But then Rob Rosenwald, a longtime fan and close friend, asked if he could have the next dance. I persuaded him to take *Drive* instead.

Rob didn't expect much more than my agent and I did. But the novel received stupendously good reviews, went almost immediately into a second printing, was picked up for paperback by a major publisher, sold in places like Russia and Japan and Finland, and got turned into an iconic movie that won Best Director at Cannes.

Go figure.

The little book I wrote mainly for fun, kicking it out of the house but thinking it would probably come back and live in my basement for the rest of its life, now has all sorts of apartments of its own all over the world.

You just never know.

1
BY ANTONIO FUSO & EMILIO LECCE

DON'T MOVE.
DON'T EVEN BREATHE.
JUST WAIT...
...AND LISTEN.
FOR SIRENS.
THE SLAM OF A CAR DOOR.
FOOTSTEPS ON THE STAIRS.

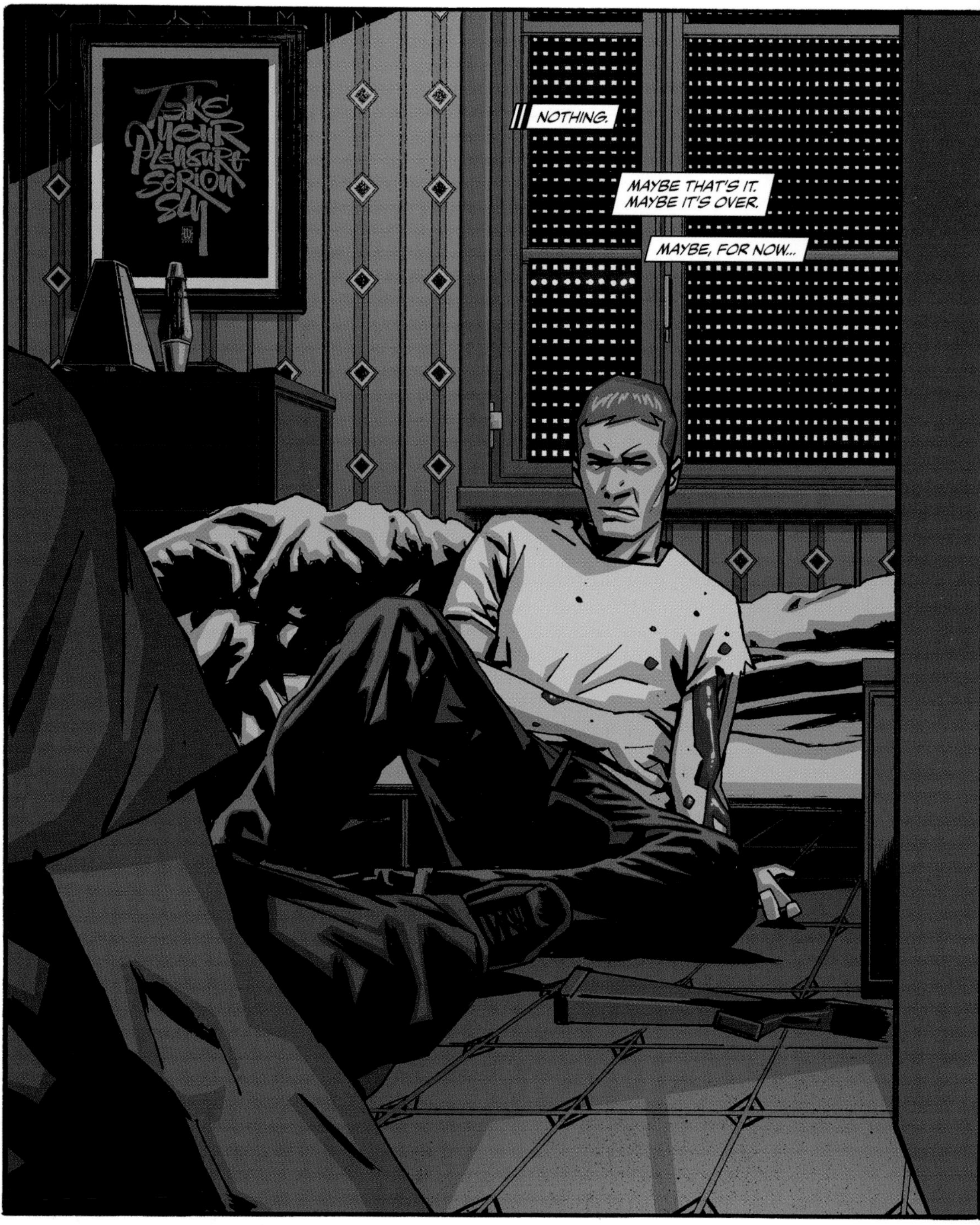
Take your pleasure seriously
NOTHING.
MAYBE THAT'S IT.
MAYBE IT'S OVER.
MAYBE, FOR NOW...

...THREE BODIES
ARE ENOUGH.

Some time earlier.
Between Sunset and Hollywood Boulevards, east of Highland.
I KNOW IT'S COOK THE SECOND HE COMES THROUGH THE DOOR.
SPEED
THANKS FOR MEETING ME HERE.
GETTING HARDER AND HARDER ALL THE TIME TO STEP AROUND THE AMATEURS. KNOW WHAT I'M SAYING?
BUT FROM WHAT I HEAR, YOU'RE THE BEST.
I AM.
OTHER THING I'VE HEARD IS, YOU CAN BE HARD TO WORK WITH.
NOT IF WE UNDERSTAND EACH OTHER.

WHAT'S TO UNDERSTAND? IT'S MY JOB. I RUN THE TEAM, CALL ALL THE SHOTS. EITHER YOU SIGN ON OR YOU DON'T.
THEN I DON'T.
FAIR ENOUGH. YOUR CALL. I DO HAVE TO WONDER, THOUGH... WHY?
I DRIVE. THAT'S ALL I DO. I DON'T SIT IN WHILE YOU'RE PLANNING THE SCORE OR WHILE YOU'RE RUNNING IT DOWN.
YOU TELL ME WHERE WE START, WHERE WE'RE HEADED, WHAT TIME OF DAY. I DON'T TAKE PART. I DON'T KNOW ANYONE. I DON'T CARRY WEAPONS.
I DRIVE.
ATTITUDE LIKE THAT HAS TO CUT DOWN SOME-THING FIERCE ON OFFERS.
IT'S NOT ATTITUDE. IT'S PRINCIPLE. I TURN DOWN A LOT MORE WORK THAN I TAKE.
YEAH, BUT THIS ONE'S SWEET.
THEY ALWAYS ARE.
NOT LIKE THIS.

COOK LAYS IT OUT FOR ME. TARGET'S A LOW-END PAWNSHOP AT THE END OF A SIXTIES STRIP MALL. SO ERRATICALLY OPEN IT DOESN'T EVEN BOTHER TO POST HOURS.
ITS REAL BUSINESS TAKES PLACE THROUGH THE BACK DOOR.
IT'S A FOUR-MAN JOB. ONLY ONE PROBLEM. IN ADDITION TO A DRIVER, COOK NEEDS A FOURTH MAN.
OKAY, ONLY TWO PROBLEMS.
THIS IS A JOKE, RIGHT?
YOU DON'T WANT TO PARTICIPATE, DON'T WANT A CUT, THERE IT IS. FEE FOR SERVICE. WE KEEP IT SIMPLE.

SORRY TO WASTE YOUR TIME.
HELP IF I ADD A ZERO?
ADD THREE.
NO ONE'S THAT GOOD.
PLENTY OF DRIVERS OUT THERE. TAKE YOUR PICK.
I THINK I JUST DID.

WHEN THE SUN GETS LOW ON THE HORIZON, ALL THE CITY'S GOOD FOLK BAIL ON JOB AND DUTY.
CALL HOME TO SEE HOW THE KIDS ARE, PLACE A BET WITH THE BOOKIE, SET UP A MEET WITH THE MISTRESS.
AND LIKE MOST CITIES...
HOTEL
...L.A. BECOMES A DIFFERENT BEAST BY NIGHT.
COOL RIDE, MAN.
HEY, WHERE YOU THINK YOU'RE GOIN'?

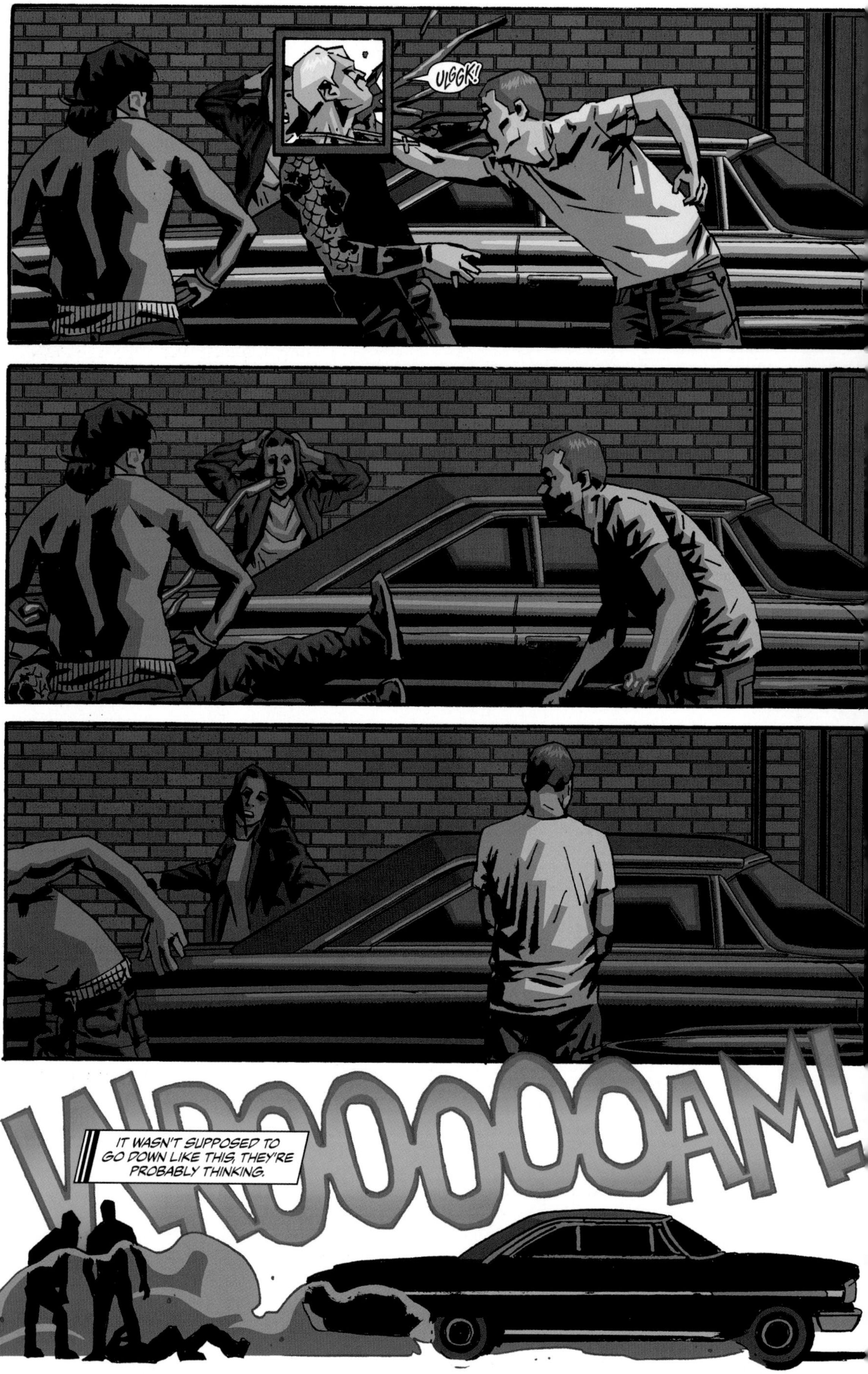
ULGGK!
VROOOOOAM!
IT WASN'T SUPPOSED TO GO DOWN LIKE THIS, THEY'RE PROBABLY THINKING.

SOMEONE SHOULD TELL THEM, THAT'S WHAT LIFE IS...
...A LONG SERIES OF THINGS THAT DON'T GO DOWN THE WAY YOU THOUGHT THEY WOULD.
HELL WITH IT. EITHER THEY'LL FIGURE IT OUT OR THEY WON'T.
MOST PEOPLE NEVER DO.

APT. FOR RENT
642-0101
HOME.
A RELATIVE TERM. I MOVE EVERY FEW MONTHS.
I FAVOR OLDER APARTMENT COMPLEXES, WHERE TENANTS LOAD UP IN THE MIDDLE OF THE NIGHT AND RIDE OFF, NEVER TO BE HEARD FROM AGAIN.
EVEN COPS DON'T LIKE COMING INTO THESE PLACES.
WHATEVER I OWN, I CAN EITHER HOIST ON MY BACK OR WALK AWAY FROM.
BEING A PART OF THE CITY AND APART FROM IT AT THE SAME TIME, THAT'S THE THING I LOVE MOST...
...THE ANONYMITY.
2-D
HELLO?

2-G
I JUST MOVED IN DOWN THE HALL. WANTED TO SAY HI.
I LIKE TO KNOW MY NEIGHBORS.
2-D
YOU'RE PROBABLY IN THE WRONG PLACE FOR THAT.
WOULDN'T BE THE FIRST TIME.
I HAVE A HISTORY OF BAD CHOICES. A DOWNRIGHT TALENT FOR THEM.
YOU NEW IN TOWN?
2-D
BEEN HERE AWHILE.
WHAT ARE YOU DOING OUT HERE IN THE PROMISED LAND?
I'M IN THE MOVIES.
SURE YOU ARE.
I'M A DRIVER... A STUNT DRIVER.

YOU MEAN ALL THOSE CAR CHASES AND STUFF?
THAT'S ME.
WOW. YOU MUST GET PAID GOOD FOR THAT.
NOT REALLY. BUT IT'S STEADY WORK.
WELL, IT'S NICE TO MEET YOU.
I'M IRINA.
I'M IN 2-G. I WORK NIGHTS, SO I'M HOME ALL DAY.
MAYBE YOU'LL COME BY SOMETIME.
2-G

SKREEEEVROOO
THAT ROCKED!
I MISSED THE LAST MARK BY HALF A YARD.
GOOD ENOUGH.
NOT FOR ME.
MAN, THIS IS WHAT?
NINETY SECONDS IN A FILM THAT LASTS TWO HOURS? NO ONE'S GONNA NOTICE.
PLENTY OF OTHER DRIVERS OUT THERE. MAKE THE CALL.

SECOND RUN. GIVE MYSELF A LITTLE MORE TIME...
SKREEE!!
...TO GET UP TO SPEED.
CLINK
SKREEEE

VROOOAM!!
SKREEEEEE!!
SKREEEE-VROOO
NICE WORK, KID! WHAT YOU THINK OF THE RIDE?
LOOKS CHERRY, BUT THE THING DRIVES LIKE A GODDAMNED MANGO.
CLAP CLAP CLAP
ON A SHOOT, I DRIVE WHATEVER THEY TELL ME TO. ON A JOB...

...I ALWAYS PICK MY OWN CAR.
BUY CARS
BUY OUT LOANS & LEASES
NEVER STEAL ONE. THAT'S THE FIRST MISTAKE PEOPLE MAKE, PROS AND AMATEURS ALIKE. I ALWAYS BUY OFF SMALL LOTS.
YOU LOOK FOR SOMETHING BLAND, MID-RANGE, SOME SHADE OF BROWN OR GRAY. SOMETHING THAT'LL FADE INTO THE BACKGROUND.
BUT YOU ALSO WANT A RIDE THAT CAN GET UP ON ITS REAR WHEELS AND PAW AIR IF YOU NEED IT TO.
THIS TIME, IT'S AN OLD DODGE. A LITTLE TOO MUCH PLAY IN THE TRANSMISSION, FEW OTHER MINOR THINGS, BUT OTHERWISE IT'S AS PERFECT AS I HAVE ANY RIGHT TO EXPECT.
I HAVE A GARAGE THAT'LL GIVE IT THE WORKS--
--NEW TIRES, OIL AND LUBE, NEW BELTS AND HOSES, A TUNE-UP--
--THEN STORE IT, WHERE IT'S OUT OF SIGHT TILL I PICK IT UP FOR THE JOB.
BUY A CAR
CAR

Some time later.
Out towards Santa Monica, near the airport.
MONEY TO LOAN
THINGS GO WRONG ON A JOB...
...SOMETIMES IT STARTS SO SUBTLY YOU DON'T SEE IT AT FIRST.
OTHER TIMES, IT'S ALL DOMINOES AND FIREWORKS.
BLAM
BLAM

DRIVE!
EEEERRRRTT

SKEEEEEEE
RAMP
40
35
VROOAM
HOOONK
M·A·N
EEEERRTT

CRASH!
DODGE
SHIT! THERE'S A LOT MORE MONEY HERE THAN THERE OUGHTA BE. HAS TO BE CLOSE TO A QUARTER OF A MILLION.
OH, SHIT.

BY ADAM GORHAM COLORS BY MICHAEL SPICER

HE A

MONDAY EDITION

ALL

REMAKE OF MODERN CLASSIC HITS THE STREETS OF L.A.

Despite the increasing costs of filming on site within the city of Los Angeles, production began this week on a remake of a classic film in several locations around the city. Few details have been officially released about the project, but eyewitnesses have reported seeing high-speed car chases through back alleys and down the streets of neighborhoods all over L.A.

"Though I can't really say much, I can tell you that there are a lot of fans out there who are going to lose it once we show them what we're working on," said a member of the film crew earlier this week. "We've all been sworn to secrecy, but watching these high-end cars roll in here the past few days has gotten everyone pretty pumped."

Many locals and onlookers have shared in the excitement as a parade of muscle cars and custom motorcycles continues to pour through the streets each day. "I've been camped out two nights now, watching everything," remarked an enthusiastic follower of the as-yet-untitled film. "And from what I've seen, this is definitely going to be the best movie of all time."

"Some of these stunt guys, these drivers, I don't know how they do it," said another eyewitness who claims to have watched the filming from a ... eighty and starts driving *backwards*. Then he darts down an alleyway and pulls another one. Dude must have been going forty, fifty miles an hour. It was *unreal*."

Others on site remarked on this particular stunt as its elaborate setup brought the action close to the area cordoned off by security personnel. The stunt driver in the scene described above emerged from his vehicle amid a frenzy of applause from the cast and crew, as well as a crowd of spectators gathered beyond the security line. The driver gave no comment as he marched past the crowd with a calm demeanor despite the intensity and danger of his actions moments earlier.

Though everyone associated with the filming has been tight-lipped, the director released a statement to the press about the project under the condition that his name ...

but I don't
than that. M
in the city
such an inte
to keep secr
people gran
vacy we're r
we deliver w
Many who h
filming seen
area locals ar
the film crew
about *my* spac
lives in the ar
blocked off en
large crowds.
enough in this
to go shutting
a *movie*? I mea

CONTINUED

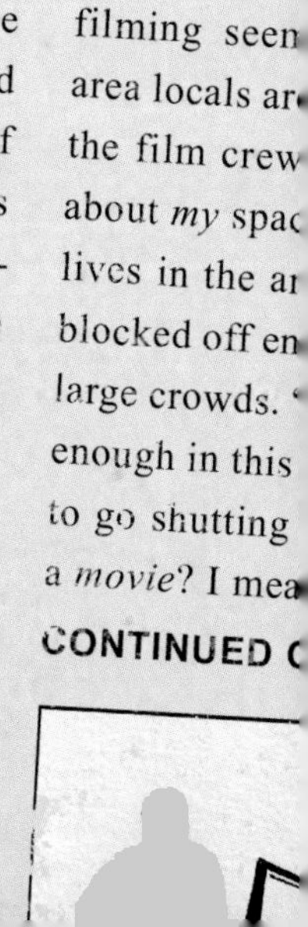

NGELS TIM

WS FROM THE CITY OF ANGELS

SE

poil any more
will be filmed
os Angeles is
of it. It's hard
town, but if
pace and pri-
I know what
th the wait."
n eye on the
e, but some
ling to grant
uest. "What
a man who
filming has
s and drawn
fic isn't bad
e guys need
ds to make
ind of...

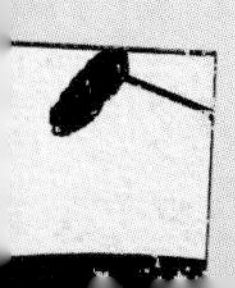

Rise in Violent Crime Possibly Linked to Criminal Organization

Violent crime has risen dramatically since last year, according to data provided by the LAPD. The Chief of Police stated this Monday that overall crime rates are up all over the city, and this increase in violent crime is driven by an overall rise in robbery and aggravated assault. Residents in all parts of the city are urged to be vigilant and aware of their surroundings, but some citizens argue that the police just aren't doing enough. "It's like a whole different city once the sun goes down," said the owner of a business near Hollywood Boulevard. "I don't feel safe going out there at night."

"The other day I saw three thugs trying to rob a young man," he continued. "They confronted him when he took out his keys to get in his car. I thought he was done for, but he fought them off and drove out of here. Two of the thugs dragged their pal away, and he was bleeding all over the place. I was horrified."

Though the Chief of Police stated on Monday that the rise in robberies and other violent crimes is not necessarily indicative of organized criminal activity, many remain skeptical. This skepticism is fueled by an investigation following a recent robbery at a pawnshop in Santa Monica. After several shots were heard, a woman was seen fleeing the shop and getting into a car waiting nearby. A high-speed chase ensued, leading to a fatal accident a short time later. Though police have released no information about the suspects' identity...

CONTINUED ON PAGE 18

Related Articles:

LAPD HESITANT TO ENTER HIGH-CRIME NEIGHBORHOODS

THE CRIMINAL NEXT DOOR: DO YOU KNOW YOUR NEIGHBORS?

FOOL

Phil's Di
can favo
stacked"
burgers sl
mix of s
made hot
ence, mak
on a bun
ocal favo
point out t
of a crowd
tell Phil! T
patties and
but delicate
throw a fit (
at complai
those who a
about his se

2
BY ANTONIO FUSO COLORS BY STEFANO SIMEONE

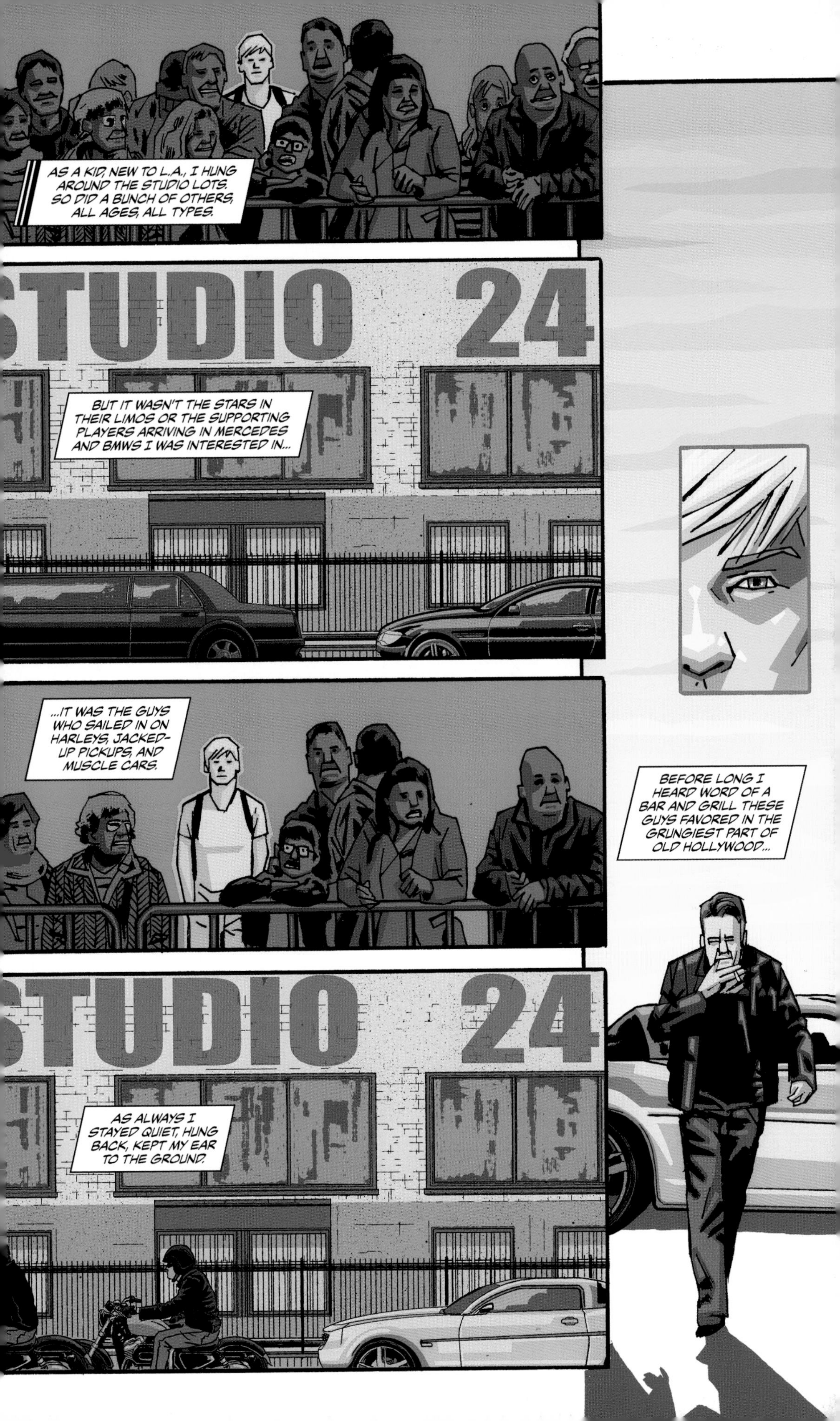
AS A KID, NEW TO L.A., I HUNG AROUND THE STUDIO LOTS. SO DID A BUNCH OF OTHERS, ALL AGES, ALL TYPES.
STUDIO 24
BUT IT WASN'T THE STARS IN THEIR LIMOS OR THE SUPPORTING PLAYERS ARRIVING IN MERCEDES AND BMWS I WAS INTERESTED IN...
...IT WAS THE GUYS WHO SAILED IN ON HARLEYS, JACKED-UP PICKUPS, AND MUSCLE CARS.
STUDIO 24
AS ALWAYS I STAYED QUIET, HUNG BACK, KEPT MY EAR TO THE GROUND.
BEFORE LONG I HEARD WORD OF A BAR AND GRILL THESE GUYS FAVORED IN THE GRUNGIEST PART OF OLD HOLLYWOOD...

...AND I STARTED HANGING OUT THERE INSTEAD.
ROCK-OLA
HI-FI
AFTERNOON, SHANNON.
KEEP 'EM COMING.
HELP YOU WITH SOMETHING, KID?
THOUGHT MAYBE I COULD BUY YOU A DRINK OR TWO.
YOU DID, DID YOU?
I'D WAGER THAT BACKPACK HOLDS DAMN NEAR EVERYTHING YOU OWN, AND LOOKS LIKE YOU HAVEN'T EATEN IN A DAY OR TWO, BUT YOU WANT TO BUY **ME** A DRINK?
YES, SIR.
YOU'LL DO JUST FINE HERE IN L.A., KID.

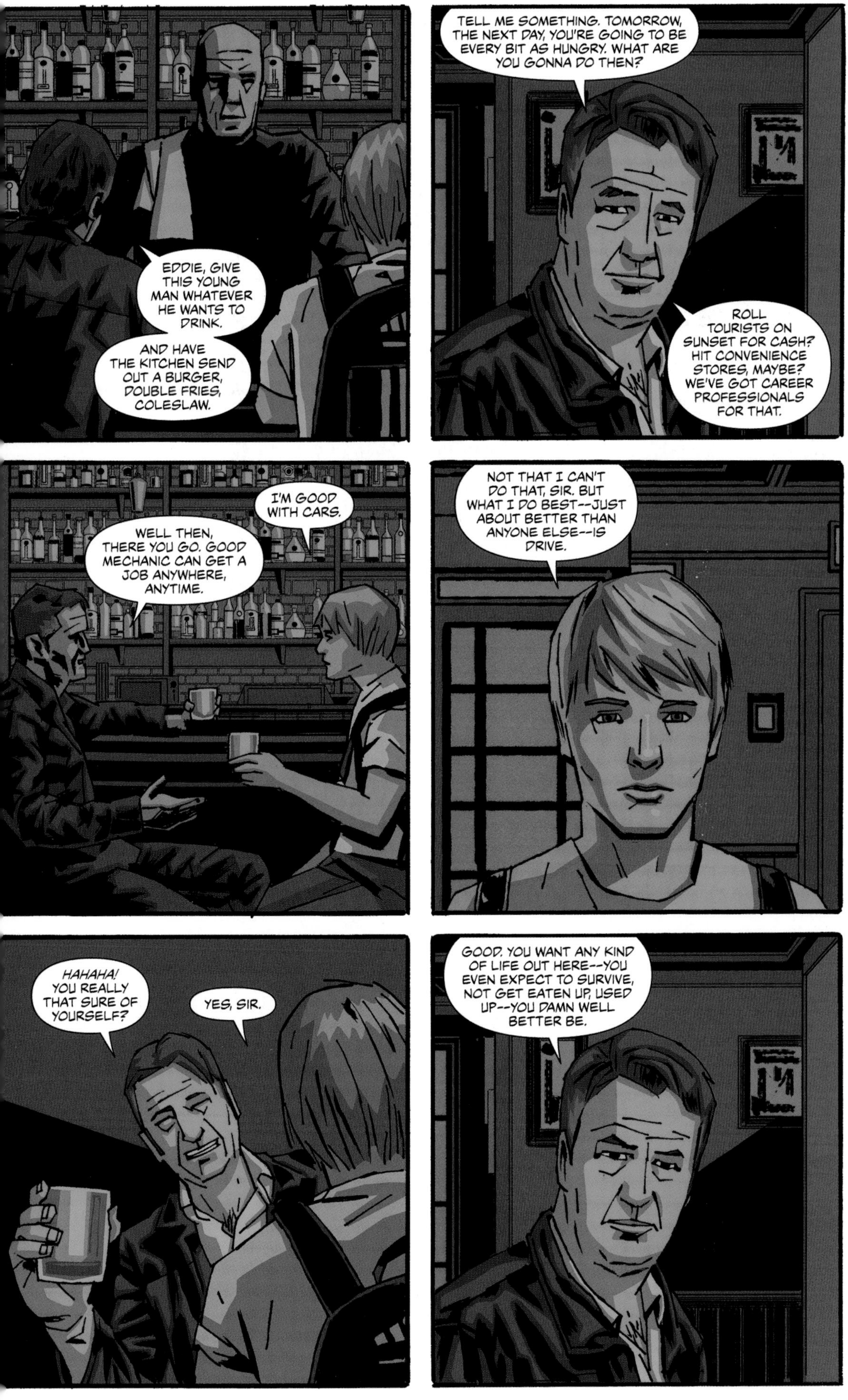
EDDIE, GIVE THIS YOUNG MAN WHATEVER HE WANTS TO DRINK.
AND HAVE THE KITCHEN SEND OUT A BURGER, DOUBLE FRIES, COLESLAW.
TELL ME SOMETHING. TOMORROW, THE NEXT DAY, YOU'RE GOING TO BE EVERY BIT AS HUNGRY. WHAT ARE YOU GONNA DO THEN?
ROLL TOURISTS ON SUNSET FOR CASH? HIT CONVENIENCE STORES, MAYBE? WE'VE GOT CAREER PROFESSIONALS FOR THAT.
I'M GOOD WITH CARS.
WELL THEN, THERE YOU GO. GOOD MECHANIC CAN GET A JOB ANYWHERE, ANYTIME.
NOT THAT I CAN'T DO THAT, SIR. BUT WHAT I DO BEST--JUST ABOUT BETTER THAN ANYONE ELSE--IS DRIVE.
HAHAHA! YOU REALLY THAT SURE OF YOURSELF?
YES, SIR.
GOOD. YOU WANT ANY KIND OF LIFE OUT HERE--YOU EVEN EXPECT TO SURVIVE, NOT GET EATEN UP, USED UP--YOU DAMN WELL BETTER BE.

HERE'S YOUR CHANCE, KID. SHOW ME WHAT YOU GOT.
VVROOOOAAAAMMMM
VVROOOOAAAAMMMM
Few years later.

LAUNDRY
LAUNDRY
MINNA
call center
SKREEE–
HOLY SHIT! PRINT THAT, NOW!
THAT'S MY BOY.

NEED ANY HELP?
I CAN MANAGE.
HOW ABOUT SOMETHING TO DRINK, THEN? HELP YOU RECOVER FROM ALL THAT HEAVY LIFTING.
THAT, I COULD DO.
2-C
SO YOU NEVER TOLD ME WHERE YOU'RE FROM.
TUCSON.
I'VE GOT SOME FAMILY LIVING OUT THERE. SOUTH TUCSON, I THINK THEY CALL IT.
THAT'S A WORLD APART, SOUTH TUCSON.
LIKE L.A. ISN'T?
YOURS?

THESE TEND TO COME WITH THE APARTMENT. PLACE IS OVERRUN WITH ROACHES AND CHILDREN.
PROBABLY WANT TO CHECK YOUR CLOSETS.
THIS IS BENICIO.
I'M FOUR!
AND VERY STUBBORN ABOUT GOING TO BED.
HOW OLD ARE YOU?
GOOD QUESTION. OKAY IF I CALL MY MOM, CHECK IN WITH HER ABOUT THIS?
MEANWHILE, WE'LL GET YOU A COOKIE AND A GLASS OF MILK OUT IN THE KITCHEN.

WELL?
HUH?
WHAT DID YOUR MOTHER SAY?
HOW OLD ARE YOU?
TWENTY, I'M AFRAID.
THAT'S OLD.
SORRY. MAYBE WE CAN STILL BE FRIENDS, THOUGH?
MAYBE.
OKAY, TIME TO TUCK YOU IN, AGAIN.

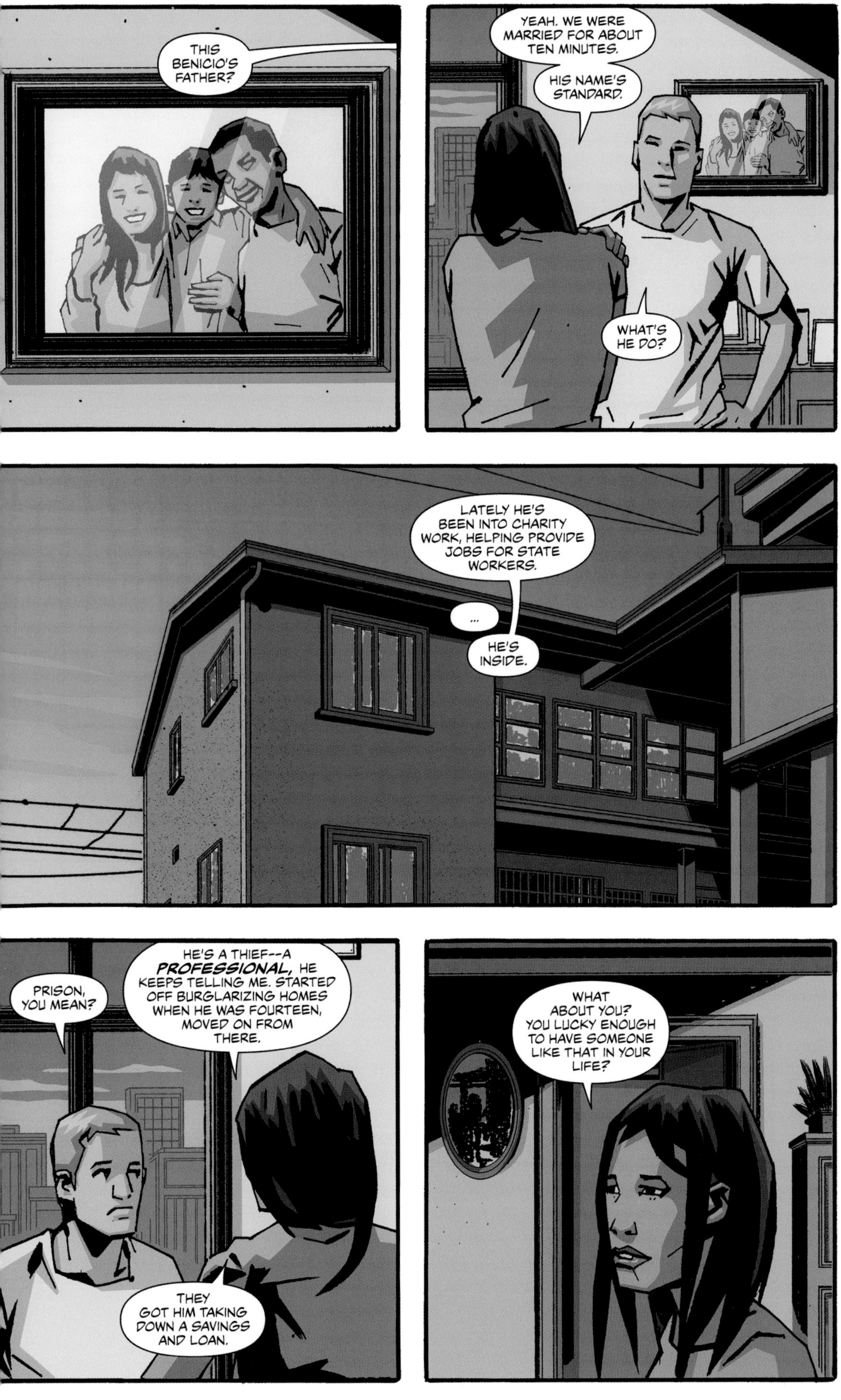
THIS BENICIO'S FATHER?
YEAH. WE WERE MARRIED FOR ABOUT TEN MINUTES.
HIS NAME'S STANDARD.
WHAT'S HE DO?
LATELY HE'S BEEN INTO CHARITY WORK, HELPING PROVIDE JOBS FOR STATE WORKERS.
...
HE'S INSIDE.
PRISON, YOU MEAN?
HE'S A THIEF--A PROFESSIONAL, HE KEEPS TELLING ME. STARTED OFF BURGLARIZING HOMES WHEN HE WAS FOURTEEN, MOVED ON FROM THERE.
THEY GOT HIM TAKING DOWN A SAVINGS AND LOAN.
WHAT ABOUT YOU? YOU LUCKY ENOUGH TO HAVE SOMEONE LIKE THAT IN YOUR LIFE?

"AS A KID, I WAS ALWAYS SMALL FOR MY AGE. COULD EASILY FIT THROUGH BATHROOM WINDOWS, PET DOORS...
"...WHICH MY FATHER TOOK FULL ADVANTAGE OF, BEING A BURGLAR.
"OTHER THAN THAT, HE HAD LITTLE USE FOR ME.
"CARED EVEN LESS FOR MY MOTHER.
"SO I WASN'T SURPRISED WHEN SHE WENT AFTER HIM ONE NIGHT AT DINNER WITH A PAIR OF KNIVES, ONE IN EACH FIST.
"WASN'T LONG AFTER THAT I STARTED HANGING AROUND A RACE TRACK OUT IN THE DESERT.
"FRIEND OF MINE--A LOCAL MECHANIC--LET ME RUN THE TRACK WITH CARS HE'D WORKED UP, WANTING TO WATCH THEIR PERFORMANCE.
"ONCE I GOT A TASTE FOR IT, I COULDN'T HOLD MYSELF BACK.

"IT WAS LIKE HER ENTIRE LIFE HAD GATHERED TOWARD THAT SINGLE, SUDDEN BOLT OF ACTION.
"SHE WASN'T GOOD FOR MUCH ELSE AFTERWARDS. I DID WHAT I COULD, BUT EVENTUALLY THE STATE CAME IN AND TOOK HER AWAY.
"ME THEY PACKED OFF TO FOSTER PARENTS--MR. AND MRS. SMITH IN TUCSON. TILL THE DAY I LEFT, THEY WERE ALWAYS SURPRISED TO SEE ME COME IN THE FRONT DOOR OR OUT OF MY ROOM.
"LATE EVENING, OUT THERE IN THE DESERT, I LEARNED A LOT OF OTHER THINGS, TOO.
"FEW DAYS SHY OF MY SIXTEENTH BIRTHDAY, I PUT EVERYTHING I OWNED IN A DUFFEL BAG AND TOOK THE SPARE KEYS TO THE SMITHS' FORD.
"AT THE END OF THEIR STREET, I TOOK A HARD LEFT TOWARD CALIFORNIA."

BY THE TIME STANDARD GOT OUT, IRINA AND BENICIO AND I WERE HANGING TOGETHER A LOT.
DIDN'T BOTHER HIM AT ALL. LONG AFTER THEY WENT TO BED, STANDARD AND I WOULD SIT OUT IN THE FRONT ROOM WATCHING TV.
LOT OF THE GOOD, OLD STUFF YOU ONLY CATCH LATE AT NIGHT.
IRINA TELLS ME YOU DRIVE... FOR THE MOVIES.
HAVE TO BE PRETTY GOOD.
I GET BY.
I'M THINKING I CAN SPEAK FRANKLY WITH YOU. YOU KNOW WHAT I DO, RIGHT?
MORE OR LESS.

OKAY. HERE'S THE THING. I'VE GOT A JOB, SOMETHING THAT'S BEEN ON THE BURNER A LONG TIME. BUT MY DRIVER'S BEEN... WELL, DETAINED. WONDERING IF THERE'S ANY CHANCE YOU'D CONSIDER TAKING HIS PLACE?
WE GO IN EARLY MORNING. IT'S--
I DON'T NEED TO KNOW, DON'T WANT TO KNOW. I'LL DRIVE FOR YOU. THAT'S ALL I'LL DO.
FAIR ENOUGH.
FIRST JOB WITH STANDARD WENT WELL...

...BUT IT WASN'T LONG BEFORE HE WAS LOOKING FOR MORE WORK. STARTED ASKING ME IF I KNEW OF ANYTHING.
THAT'S WHAT LED ME BACK TO COOK.
...SCORE'S SET FOR NINE TOMORROW MORNING, JUST AFTER OPENING.
ZLATAN LOUNGE BAR
SO WE HAVE A DEAL. YOU GUYS UP FOR ANOTHER SHOT?
C'MON, BLANCHE. GIVE ME A HAND.
WAY IT LOOKS, WE'RE IN AND OUT IN FIVE, SIX MINUTES TOPS. HALF AN HOUR LATER, WE'RE SITTING OVER A LUNCH OF PRIME RIB.
RIGHT.
I EVER TELL YOU HOW MUCH BENICIO DEPENDS ON YOU? IRINA THINKS THE WORLD OF YOU, TOO.
YOU KNOW THAT, RIGHT?
BOTH SENTIMENTS ARE FULLY RETURNED.
SAY SOMETHING HAPPENED TO ME... THINK YOU MIGHT SEE YOUR WAY CLEAR TO TAKING CARE OF THEM?
YEAH... YEAH, I'D DO THAT.
GOOD.

EVERYTHING STARTED OUT FINE. ACCORDING TO PLAN.
WE WENT IN AT NINE, FIRST OPENING. SEEMS AGES AGO NOW.
THREE WENT IN...
...ONLY ONE CAME OUT, AND IT WASN'T STANDARD.
AFTER EVERYTHING WENT TO HELL, THE TWO OF US CAME HERE. I KEEP RUNNING THE SCRIPT IN MY HEAD.
IT WAS A SET UP. NO OTHER WAY THAT CAR WAS DOWN THERE WAITING FOR US.
HAS TO BE BLANCHE.
WHAT?

CHOOM

CRAS

HRRRK!
AAAAGGGLC
GGHHH !!
THOOM THOOM THOOM

BLAM!

ARM HURTS LIKE A SON OF A BITCH. WORRY ABOUT THAT LATER. FOR NOW...
...DON'T MOVE.
DON'T EVEN BREATHE.
JUST WAIT... AND LISTEN...

BY ANTONIO FUSO COLORS BY JASON LEWIS

BREAKING INTO HOLLYWOOD, THE RISE OF THE HEIST MOVIE

In a city of so many trying to break into the film industry, how do aspiring actors, writers, and directors get their shot to prove themselves? There is no denying that good looks and the right connections can get you far in Hollywood, but that's not all it takes. Call it persistence, perseverance, tenacity, or what have you—sticking around till the bitter end and seeing your job through to the finish can be the difference between life and death, professionally speaking.

"In the old days, even if you were a great actor, writer, whatever but no one'd seen your stuff, it didn't matter," said an agent associated with a local talent search website. "You used to have to wait around studio lots all day hoping to get noticed. But that *never* works! Now, you can just throw whatever you've done up on the Internet, and boom, you've got an instant audience. So long as you have a final product, someone'll watch it."

So besides stick-to-itiveness—and of course a lot of luck—what else can give you a leg up against the competition? Well, research is key, say industry professionals. Following trends and knowing what the next big thing is can make a world of difference, and if you can figure that out before anyone else, you've got a golden ticket. No matter who you are in Hollywood, chasing the next big trend is par for the course.

Whether it's disaster movies, rehashed fantasy teen dramas, or a remake on an old classic, being in the right place at the right time and releasing your work ahead of the pack gets you noticed. But even if you're not a trendsetting visionary, jumping on the bandwagon and doing the same job better than the others out there can be just as good.

That begs the question, what's hot

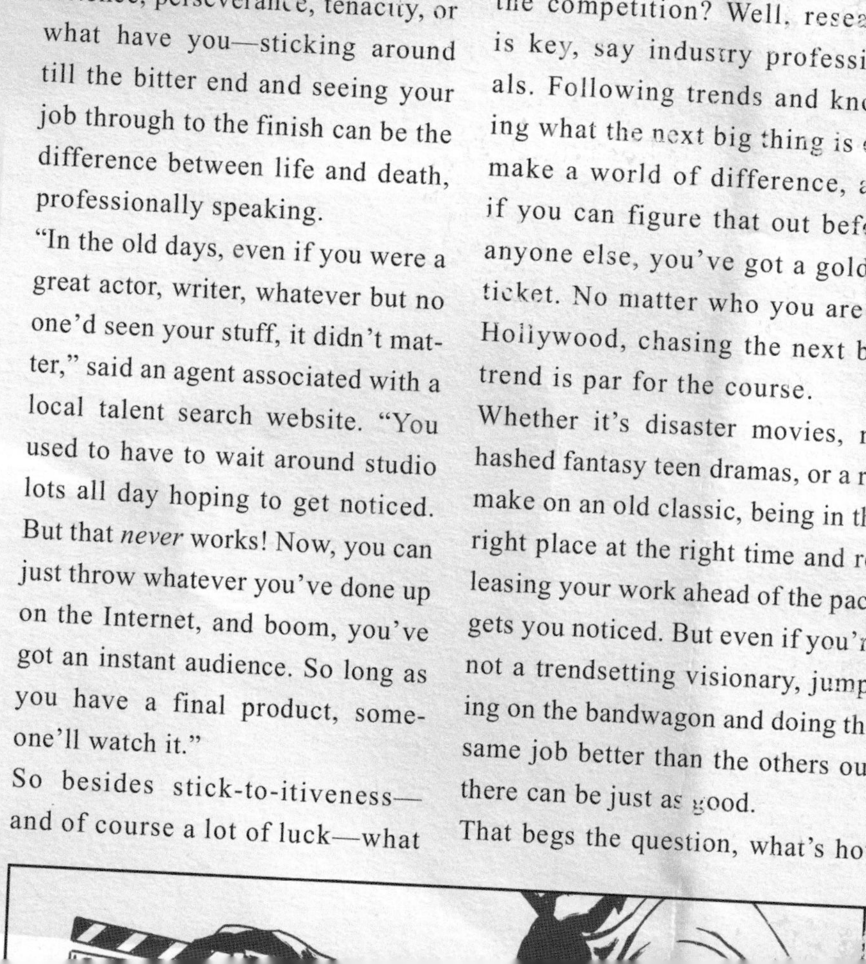

NGELS TIMES
THE NEWS FROM THE CITY OF ANGELS

in Tinseltown? The an-
movies. Just about every
ms to be plotting their
e caper, and dozens of
es are in production now,
dy to flood the market
er.
loves heist movies. They
ting the dots. They want
it's done—they need to
l to know. It's like a
award-winning director
ntino in a recent inter-
s what's so cool about
ject. It's a futurized
er revenge drama—but
tantly, it's a heist
though you never re-
heist. Anyway, it's a
up that's never been
territory in the history
a groundbreaking epic
ultaneously transcend
e medium."

No Hope for Ex-Cons in City of Angels

A study released by the California Corrections and Rehabilitation Organization this week contained some shocking statistics regarding ex-offenders within the city of Los Angeles. Home to a disproportionately large population of convicted felons and former prisoners within the state, L.A. County does little to provide assistance to individuals who are desperately seeking employment after paying their debt to society.

The strongest indicator of whether someone released from prison will return to the community as a functional, law-abiding citizen depends heavily on employment opportunities. Former inmates who manage to secure steady jobs are not only able to obtain housing and numerous other tangible benefits for themselves and their families, there is also an immeasurable gain in confidence and emotional wellbeing.

For those who cannot find work, a return to a life of crime is far more likely and, some clai
of the only options. Thoug
eral California non-profit o
zations work tirelessly to
the playing field, more ne
be done by owners of both
and small businesses withi
city of Los Angeles. Most
ployment forms require a
cants to divulge whether
have ever been convicted
crime, and more often than
these applications are imm
ately dismissed or moved to
bottom of the pile.

Without the opportunity to ente
workforce at any level, ex-offen
are often forced to fall back on
few connections they have, and
younger men and women, their
tions are even fewer. Without a
sirable skillset or significant w
history, there is a very low cha
any employer will look past a pre
ous conviction.

"I'm not proud of what I did, b
I've paid my dues. I love my w
and son for standing by me, a
now it's time for me to make rig
by them," said recently released

CONTINUED ON PAGE 12

Related Articles:

**LAPD TURNS UP NO CLUES I
HOTEL SHOOTOUT**

**L.A. DRAINAGE CANALS BONE DRY
FLOODED WITH ILLEGAL ACTIVITY**

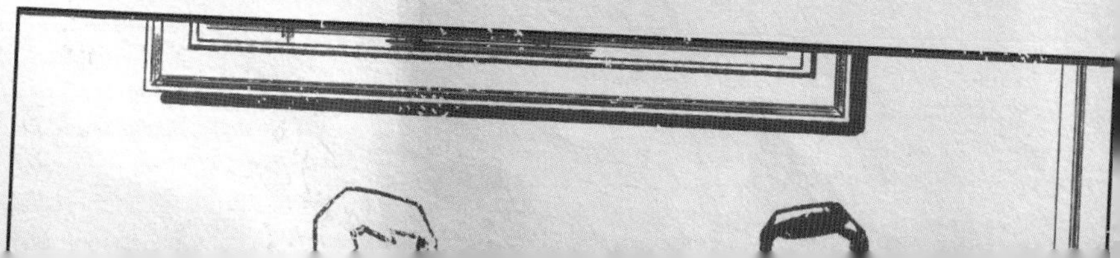

3
BY ANTONIO FUSO COLORS BY STEFANO SIMEONE

GARAGE
OIL CHANGES ALWAYS FREE!
KNOCK KNOCK
YOU'RE DRIPPING ON MY WELCOME MAT.
YOU DON'T HAVE A WELCOME MAT.
NO--BUT I USED TO. A NICE ONE. THEN PEOPLE SOMEHOW STARTED GETTING THE NOTION I MEANT IT.
YOU COULD BE THE BLOODMAN, YOU KNOW. LIKE THE MILK-MAN. MAKING DELIVERIES. HALF A PINT OF SERUM, TWO PINTS OF WHOLE. I DON'T NEED ANY BLOOD, BLOODMAN.

BUT I WILL... AND A LOT MORE IF YOU DON'T LET ME IN.
THAT ARM DOESN'T LOOK SO GOOD. YOU WANT, I COULD HAVE A LOOK AT IT.
I DIDN'T CALL AHEAD.
NAPA AutoCare Center
I'LL WORK YOU IN. BE GOOD TO BE OF USE AGAIN.

EYESIGHT'S NOT WHAT IT USED TO BE. THEN AGAIN, WHAT IS?
MEDICINE WAS THE GREAT LOVE OF MY LIFE, BUT IT'S BEEN A WHILE.
SURE HOPE I REMEMBER THE HOW OF IT.
RELAX. JUST HAVING MY FUN WITH YOU.
TAKE A FEW HITS OF THIS, BOY. CHANCES ARE YOU'LL NEED IT. PROBABLY BOTH OF US WILL BEFORE THIS IS OVER.
Mad Label
YOU READY?
JUST ABOUT.

Few Days Later.
I KNEW ONCE THE HARD BOYS FROM THE HOTEL DIDN'T COME HOME, WHOEVER SENT THEM WOULD BE SENDING SOMEONE IN AFTER. TOO MANY LOOSE ENDS WHIPPING AROUND IN THE WIND.
SO I TOOK THE KEYS OFF THE FAT MAN STUCK IN THE WINDOW. TOOK THEIR CHEVY. MOVED IT WHERE IT WOULD BE HARD BUT NOT TOO HARD TO FIND.

MasterCharge
ONLY THING LEFT TO DO IS WAIT CLOSE BY, THINK THINGS OVER.
WiFi

SOMEONE SET US ALL UP. LITTLE DOUBT ABOUT THAT NOW.
STANDARD I KNEW I COULD TRUST. I BROUGHT HIM IN, AND HE DIDN'T MAKE IT OUT.
BLANCHE COULD HAVE BEEN IN FROM THE FIRST, BUT IT DIDN'T FEEL THAT WAY. NOT THAT IT MATTERS NOW.
AND COOK. MAYBE HE'D BEEN PART OF THE SET-UP. MAYBE LIKE THE REST OF US, ONLY A BOARD PIECE, A SHILL.
EITHER WAY, EVENTUALLY SOMEONE'S GOING TO COME LOOKING FOR THE CHEVY. MAKING THE QUESTION...

...WHO'S LIKELY TO SHOW?

SORRY, BUT THE SHOTGUN'S NOT MUCH USE ANYMORE.
THONK

LETON
KE
Apple Pies
coffee
Drink
BLANCHE ISN'T MUCH GOOD, EITHER.
WiFi
YOU'RE SUPPOSED TO BE DEAD.

WHOSE MONEY DO I HAVE, COOK?
HRRK HRRK
TELL ME.
GKKK... NI--NINO... GKKK...

STUMP
Nino's
Pizza
we deliver

RRRING... RRRING... RRRING...
NINO'S PIZZA. WE'RE NOT OPEN. CALL BACK AFTER ELEVEN.
TELEPHO
NEED TO TALK TO NINO. SEEMS I HAVE SOMETHING OF HIS.
AND THAT WOULD BE...?
CLOSE TO A QUARTER OF A MILLION DOLLARS.
PLEASE HOLD.
NINO HERE. WHO THE *FUCK* IS THIS? YOU *HAVE* SOMETHING OF MINE?
YEAH. I HAVEN'T COUNTED, BUT BLANCHE TOLD ME THERE'S SOMETHING OVER TWO HUNDRED GRAND IN THE BAG.
THERE ***DAMN WELL BETTER BE.*** AND YOU'RE TELLING ME THIS ***BECAUSE?***
BECAUSE IT'S YOUR MONEY, YOUR BAG. SAY THE WORD, BOTH CAN BE AT YOUR DOOR TOMORROW.

...YOU'RE NOT VERY GOOD AT THIS, ARE YOU?
AT WHAT I DO, I'M THE BEST. THIS ISN'T WHAT I DO.
I CAN SEE THAT. SO WHAT DO YOU GET OUT OF IT?
JUST THAT, OUT OF IT.
ONCE THE MONEY'S IN YOUR HANDS, WE'RE EVEN.
YOU FORGET ME, FORGET ABOUT COOK, FORGET WE EVER HAD THIS CONVERSATION...
WE HAVE A DEAL?
YEAH. WE HAVE A DEAL. LOOKS LIKE YOU KNOW WHERE TO FIND ME.
FIND THIS GUY--I DON'T CARE HOW--AND TAKE CARE OF HIM. THERE CAN'T BE ANYONE WHO KNOWS ABOUT THIS.
YOU GOT IT.

ISOLATED SPOT, OUT BY THE WATER.
I WAIT TILL AFTER DARK...
...TO SAY GOODBYE TO COOK.

I COULD TELL NINO'S NOT ONE TO JUST LET THINGS LIE.
AND AFTER I HIT THE STREETS, IT DOESN'T TAKE LONG FOR ME TO SPOT SOMEONE TAILING ME, LODGED IN MY REAR-VIEW MIRROR.
HE'S HANGING BACK...
...BUT HE WON'T SHAKE.
DODGE

STILL, CAN'T LEAD HIM BACK TO MY PLACE.
BRRRNT
SO THAT JUST LEAVES THE ONE OPTION.

ERRRT
SKREE –
– SKEEE
BRRRRT

BRRRRNT
KRASH

APT. FOR RENT
642-0101
SOONER OR LATER, THEY WERE GOING TO COME AFTER ME.
2-G
IT WAS ONLY A MATTER OF TIME, BUT--
IRINA! BENICIO!
2-G

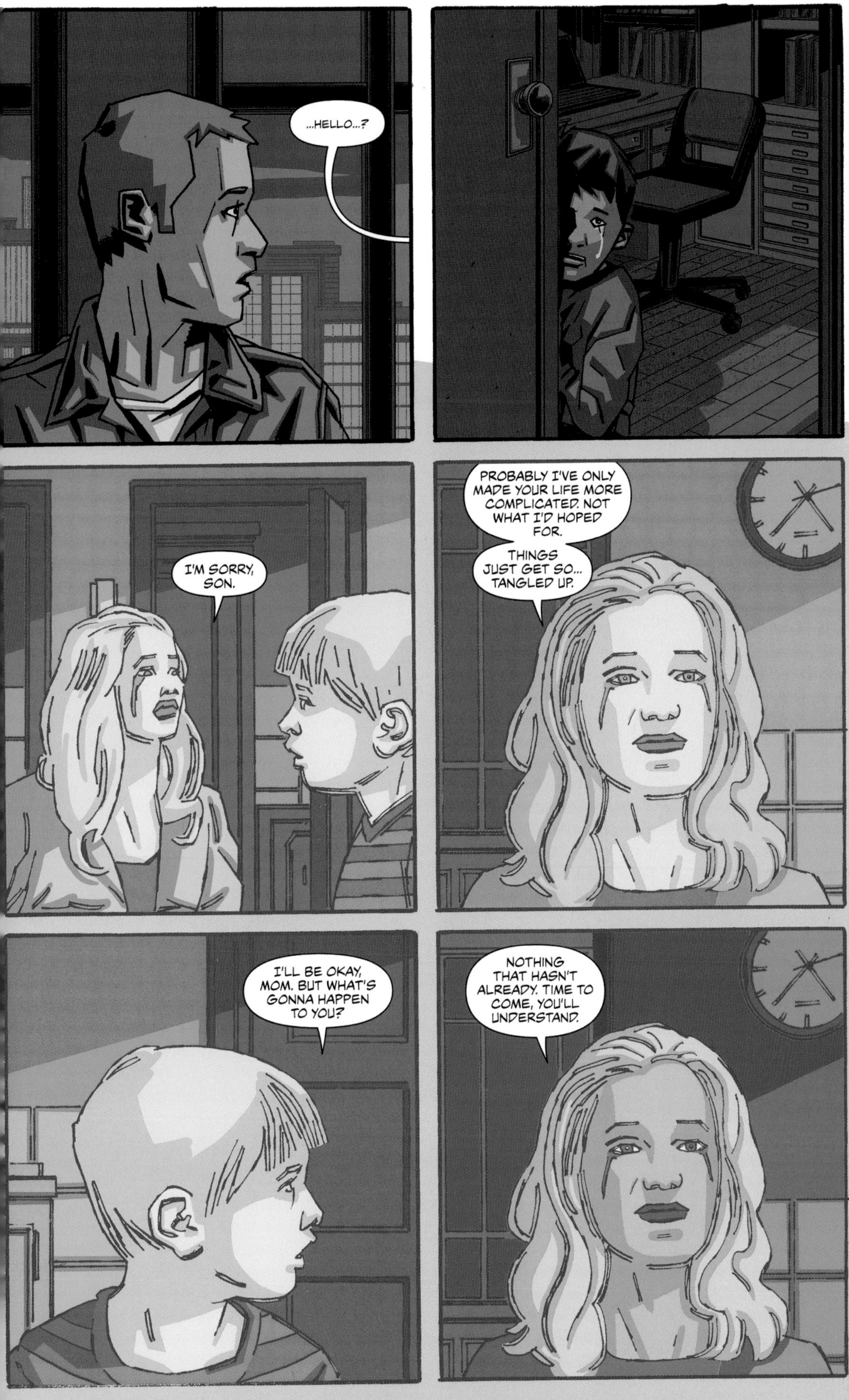
...HELLO...?
I'M SORRY, SON.
PROBABLY I'VE ONLY MADE YOUR LIFE MORE COMPLICATED. NOT WHAT I'D HOPED FOR.
THINGS JUST GET SO... TANGLED UP.
I'LL BE OKAY, MOM. BUT WHAT'S GONNA HAPPEN TO YOU?
NOTHING THAT HASN'T ALREADY. TIME TO COME, YOU'LL UNDERSTAND.

BY ANTONIO FUSO COLORS BY JASON LEWIS

THURSDAY EDITION

AI

The Hor

Still No Suspects in Triple Hotel Homicide

The Los Angeles Police Department has released no new information regarding possible suspects in the recent mid-day shootout that left three dead and many hotel patrons stunned. Eyewitnesses reported seeing two armed men force their way into an occupied room. Gunshots were heard, and an injured white male was seen exiting the room soon after. The suspect quickly fled the scene. Though several eyewitnesses spoke with officers after the events, conflicting reports have left detectives with little concrete information.

String of Break-Ins Ends with Young Mother's Death

A series of burglaries at an apartment complex in Echo Park ended with the death of a young woman two nights ago. The victim's four-year-old son was present during the time of the break-in, but he was uninjured and is now safe with extended family, according to a report filed by Los Angeles Police Department Detective Gil Franks.

"Two residences were broken into," said Franks, "and the suspects went through each room. Tore the places apart, but they didn't take anything. We believe they were looking for something specific and that this may have been a targeted incident. No information about the woman or her son's whereabouts will be released at this time."

An anonymous call was made to the police, reporting the break-in and murder shortly after they occurred. The deceased's four-year-old son was brought to the police station on W 6th Street, but the individual who brought the child fled before speaki...

ge

Death i Vehicul

A tractor-
and anoth
Angeles P
for the dri
sedan. The
sustained o
with anoth
the cause o

NGELES TIMES

NEWS FROM THE CITY OF ANGELS

cide Report

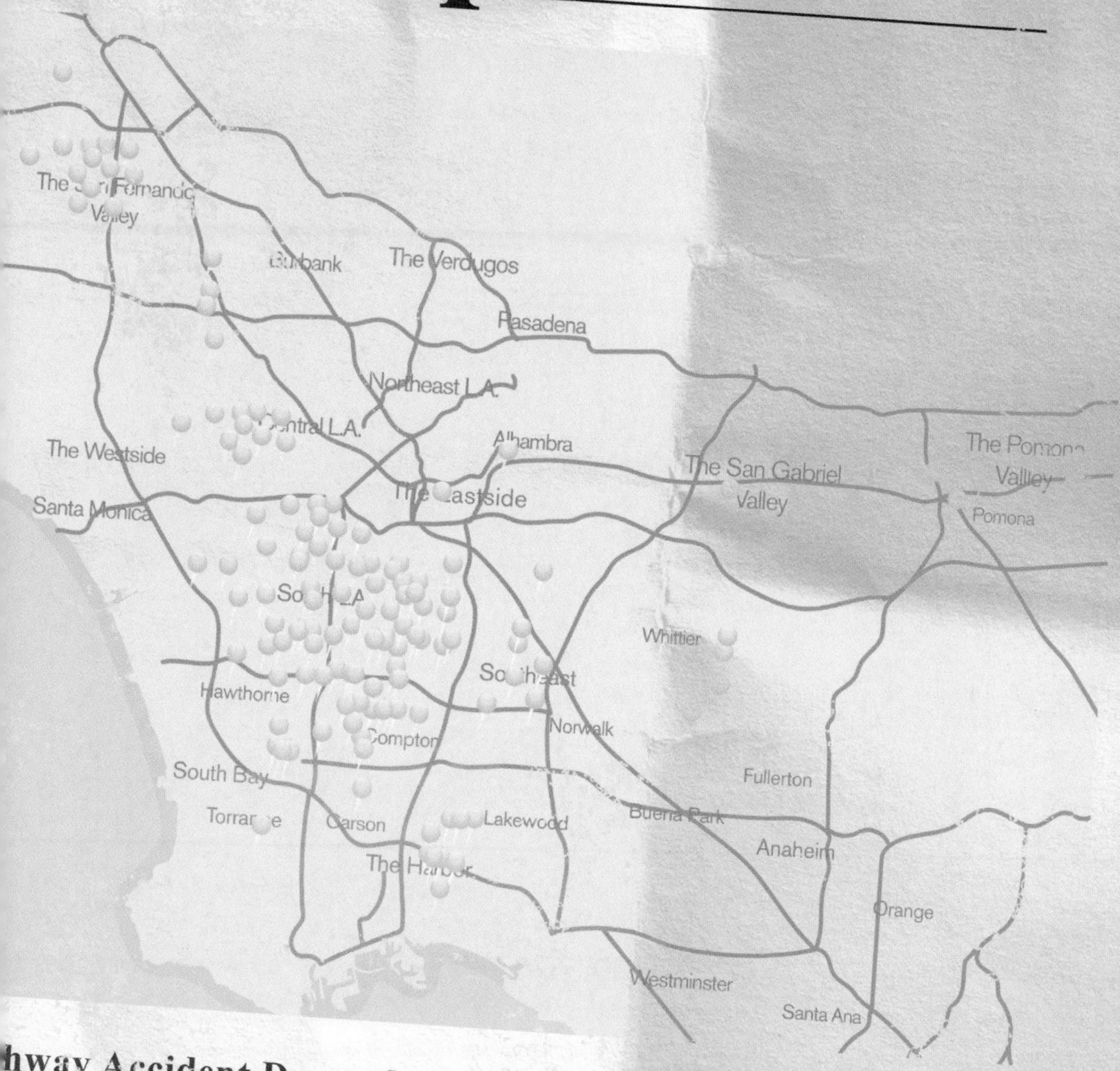

hway Accident Deemed micide

collision that left one dead ed on Interstate 405 has Los epartment officials searching red and black four-door of the tractor-trailer, who nor injuries after colliding le, claims a third driver was cident.

Suspected Murder Victim Discovered in Long Beach Harbor

The body of an unidentified man was discovered by a group of dockworkers in Long Beach Harbor early yesterday morning. The Los Angeles County Coroner reports the man died of asphyxia due to strangulation prior to entering the water. Police found no identification on the deceased and suspect the death may be related to the recent rise

BY ANTONIO FUSO COLORS BY STEFANO SIMEONE

Nino's Pizza
ITALIAN KITCHEN
YEAH, YEAH. I HEAR YA. I'LL BE BACK IN A MINUTE.
BUNCHA ASSHOLES.
WHAT THE--

ONE OF THE COOKS CAME OUT TO EMPTY THE GREASE TRAPS AND TRIPPED OVER HIM.
GODDAMN. WHAT A WAY TO GO.
BOY'S GONE. NO DOUBT ABOUT IT.
COULDN'T HAVE BEEN LONG. HOW FAR AWAY COULD THE SON OF A BITCH HAVE GOTTEN?
WHOEVER HE IS, HE'S GOTTEN TOO CLOSE.
LET'S GO TALK TO NINO.

SO YOU'VE SICCED THE HOUNDS ON THIS GUY, AND THE FIRST I HEAR OF IT IS WHEN HE STEPS UP IN MY OWN BACKYARD...
GOOD THING THERE'S NO UNION FOR OUR KIND OF WORK, NINO.
THAT'S MY BUSINESS, AND YOU DAMN WELL KNOW IT IS.
TRUST ME. THIS WAS OFF TO THE SIDE, NOT BUSINESS AS USUAL. MADE SENSE TO FARM IT OUT.
OFF TO THE SIDE'S THE SORT OF THING GETS YOU TAKEN DOWN, NINO. YOU KNOW THAT.
TIMES ARE CHANGING.
TIMES ARE FOR DAMN SURE CHANGING WHEN YOU SEND AMATEURS OUT ON A KILL AND DON'T EVEN BOTHER TO LET YOUR OWN PARTNER KNOW WHAT'S GOING ON.
I FUCKED UP. BELIEVE ME, I KNOW IT. I SHOULD HAVE BROUGHT YOU IN, BUT I'LL TAKE CARE OF IT.
SO YOU'RE GONNA DO WHAT? DISPATCH MORE OF YOUR AMATEURS?
THEY WOULDN'T BE AMATEURS.
THEY'RE ALL AMATEURS NOWADAYS. ALL OF 'EM. CARBON COPIES WITH THEIR GODDAMN TATTOOS AND CUTE LITTLE EARRINGS.

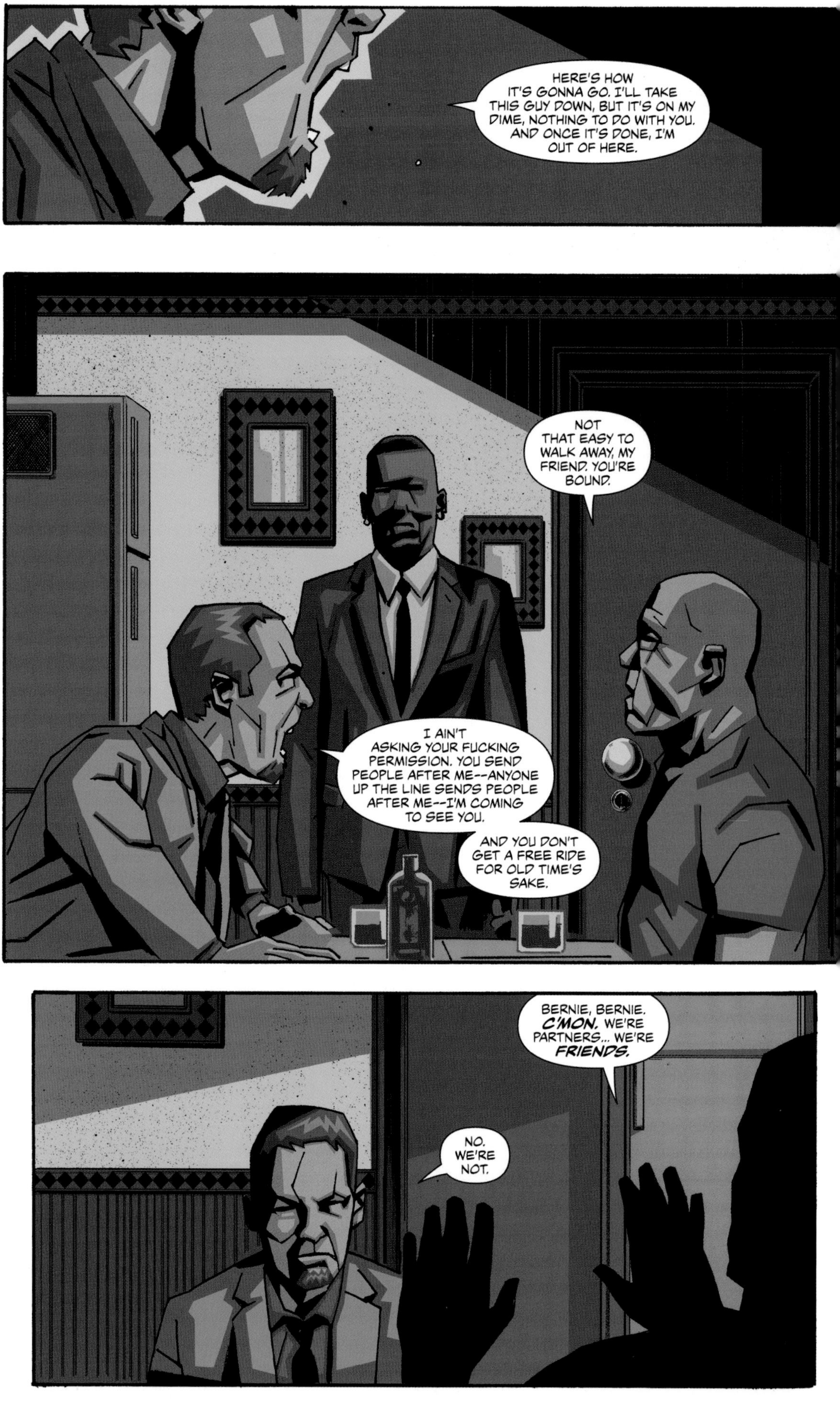
HERE'S HOW IT'S GONNA GO. I'LL TAKE THIS GUY DOWN, BUT IT'S ON MY DIME, NOTHING TO DO WITH YOU. AND ONCE IT'S DONE, I'M OUT OF HERE.
NOT THAT EASY TO WALK AWAY, MY FRIEND. YOU'RE BOUND.
I AIN'T ASKING YOUR FUCKING PERMISSION. YOU SEND PEOPLE AFTER ME--ANYONE UP THE LINE SENDS PEOPLE AFTER ME--I'M COMING TO SEE YOU.
AND YOU DON'T GET A FREE RIDE FOR OLD TIME'S SAKE.
BERNIE, BERNIE. *C'MON.* WE'RE PARTNERS... WE'RE *FRIENDS.*
NO. WE'RE NOT.

Nino's Pizza
ITALIAN KITCHEN
BLIP
BLIP
Nino's Pizza
ITALIAN KITCHEN
SKREE
Nino's Pizza
ITALIAN KITCHEN
Nino's Pizza
ITALIAN KITCHEN
Nino's Pizza
ITALIAN KITCHEN

DAMN IT, NINO. WE COME OUT HERE TO WONDERLAND, AND YOU START THINKING YOU'RE SOME KIND OF GODDAMN PRODUCER. WHAT'S SO WRONG WITH JUST BEING A GOOD MAINTENANCE MAN?
ALL THIS UNWARRANTED AMBITION, IT'S IN THE WATER AND AIR OUT HERE, IN THE GODDAMN POUNDING SUNLIGHT. LIKE A VIRUS.
IT GETS INTO YOU AND WON'T LET GO.
OKAY. RUN IT DOWN.
NINO SET UP THE GRAB, OR MORE LIKELY, FARMED IT OUT. DIRECTOR PUT A TEAM TOGETHER AND BROUGHT IN THE DRIVER. SHOULDN'T BE TOO HARD TO STEP IN THOSE FOOTPRINTS, TRACK THIS GUY DOWN.
Robertson Blvd
Culver City
3/4 MILE
ONCE THAT'S DONE, I CAN CLEAN UP THE MESS NINO MADE BEFORE THIS GUY SHOWS UP AT MY DOOR.
BUT THIS IS THE LAST DAMN TIME.

COUPLE NEXT DOOR ARE AT IT AGAIN.
KNOCK KNOCK
I'M SICK OF LISTENING TO THIS.
HI. BERNIE ROSE, NEXT APARTMENT--
I KNOW, I KNOW. WHAT'S UP? I'M KIND OF BUSY HERE.
I HEARD.
HEY!
LISTEN! YOU CAN'T JUST--
YOU ALL RIGHT, SHONDA?

HRRK
THMP
I'M A PATIENT MAN, LENNY. NOT MUCH FOR GETTING IN OTHER PEOPLE'S WAY. WHAT I FIGURE IS, WE'VE ALL GOT OUR OWN LIVES AND THE RIGHT TO BE LEFT ALONE.
SO I SIT OVER THERE FOR ALMOST A YEAR NOW LISTENING TO WHAT GOES ON IN HERE, AND I KEEP THINKING, HEY, HE'S A MENSCH, HE'LL WORK IT OUT.
YOU GONNA WORK IT OUT, LENNY?
YEAH, SURE.
SHONDA'S A GOOD WOMAN. YOU'RE LUCKY TO HAVE HER, LUCKY SHE'S PUT UP WITH YOU THIS LONG, LUCKY *I'VE* PUT UP WITH YOU.
SHE HAS GOOD REASON. SHE LOVES YOU...
...I DON'T HAVE ANY REASON AT ALL.

WELL, THAT WAS STUPID. I'M GETTING SLOPPY.
LETTING MY EMOTIONS GET THE BETTER OF ME.
SEEN THIS HAPPEN TO GUYS BEFORE. THEY BURNOUT, START WONDERING WHAT IT IS THEY'RE DOING, WHY ANY OF IT MATTERS. THEN THEY DISAPPEAR NOT LONG AFTER.
GET SENT UP FOR A LIFETIME HAUL, KILLED BY SOMEONE THEY'VE BRACED, OR GET TAKEN DOWN BY THEIR OWN PEOPLE.
I'M NOT GOING OUT LIKE THAT. THAT'S NOT ME. I'M NO BURNOUT.
Nino's
we deliver
THIS DRIVER FOR DAMN SURE ISN'T.
I HATE FUCKING PIZZA.

DROVE ALL DAY. NOWHERE IN PARTICULAR. JUST KNOW I CAN'T GO BACK. HOURS BEFORE I REALIZED WHERE I WAS HEADED...
...EVEN LONGER BEFORE I KNEW WHY.
BEEN YEARS SINCE I'VE BEEN OUT HERE.
WELCOME TUCSON
CITY LIMITS
BICYCLE Friendly COMMUNITY
AND IT STILL LOOKS JUST LIKE I REMEMBER.

PLACES LIKE THIS, THESE LITTLE POCKETS OF EXISTENCE, NOTHING MUCH EVER CHANGES.
I'M SURE THE SMITHS ARE JUST THE SAME.
ORDINARY LIFE LIKE THEIRS, IT WAS NEVER FOR ME. I WAS TRYING TO GET OUT FROM DAY ONE.
LIFE BY DEFINITION IS UPSET--AGITATION, CONSTANT MOVEMENT.
VROOOAM
BUT I'VE GOT A FEW MORE THINGS LEFT TO DO BEFORE I MOVE ON.
I always Felt bad about
taking your car when
I left.
Never doubt I appreciate
what you did For me.
please accept this money
in gratitude.
ou deserve to spend the
est of your lives in
ecurity

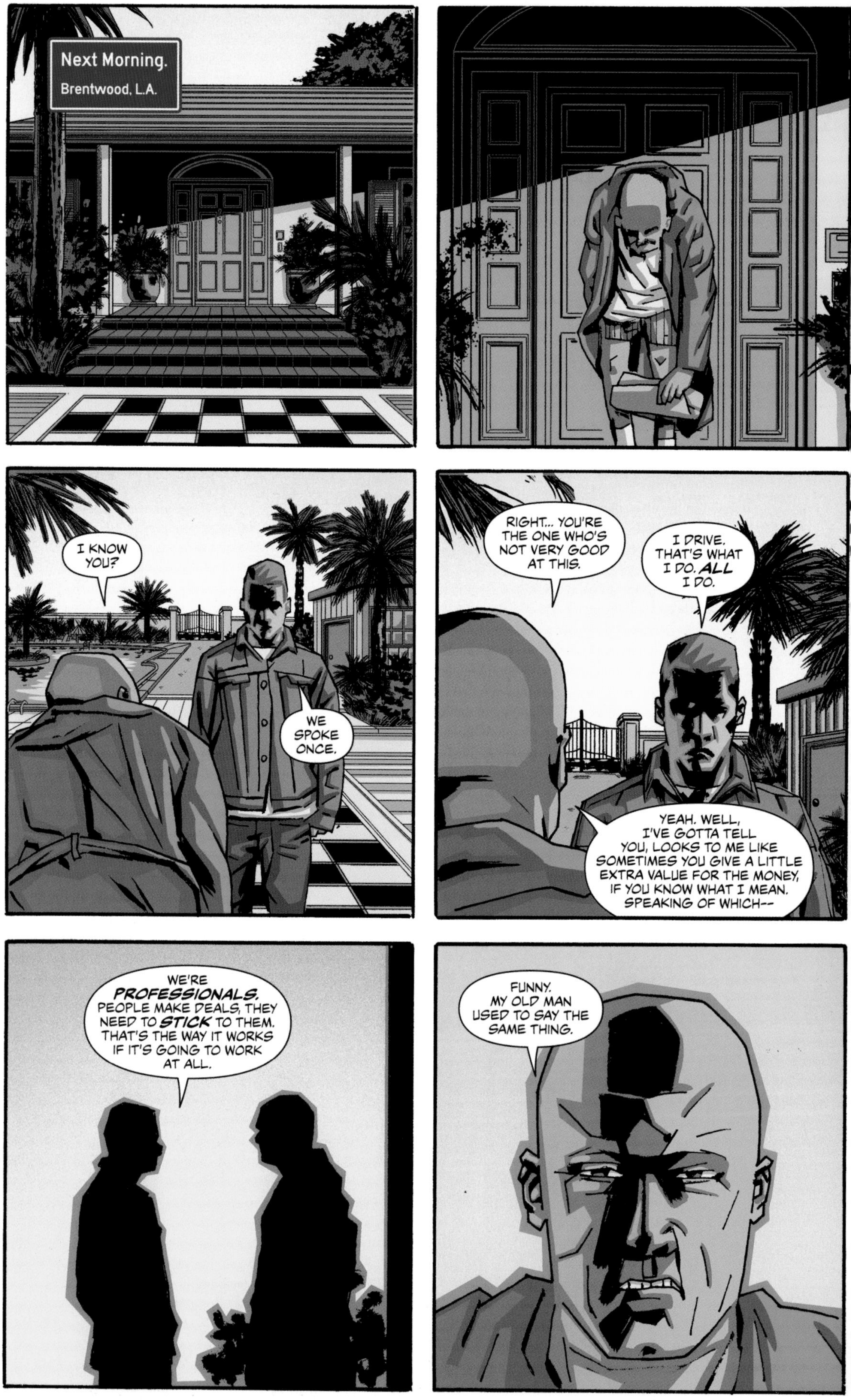
Next Morning.
Brentwood, L.A.
I KNOW YOU?
WE SPOKE ONCE.
RIGHT... YOU'RE THE ONE WHO'S NOT VERY GOOD AT THIS.
I DRIVE. THAT'S WHAT I DO. ALL I DO.
YEAH. WELL, I'VE GOTTA TELL YOU, LOOKS TO ME LIKE SOMETIMES YOU GIVE A LITTLE EXTRA VALUE FOR THE MONEY, IF YOU KNOW WHAT I MEAN. SPEAKING OF WHICH--
WE'RE PROFESSIONALS. PEOPLE MAKE DEALS, THEY NEED TO STICK TO THEM. THAT'S THE WAY IT WORKS IF IT'S GOING TO WORK AT ALL.
FUNNY. MY OLD MAN USED TO SAY THE SAME THING.

PFFT
YOU SHOULD'VE LISTENED TO HIM.
PFFT
PFFT
PFFT

RIIING RIIING
HELLO...?
IT'S DONE.
WHAT?
NINO. EARLY THIS MORNING.
HIS FAMILY?
ALL STILL ASLEEP.
YEAH. NINO NEVER SLEPT MUCH. I USED TO TELL HIM IT WAS A BAD CONSCIENCE. HE CLAIMED HE NEVER HAD ONE.
YOU DON'T SEEM SURPRISED.
GIVEN THE CIRCUMSTANCES, I ASSUMED IT WAS COMING. SOONER RATHER THAN LATER.
GUESS THAT JUST LEAVES THE TWO OF US. FIGURE IT'S TIME WE MET. YOU KNOW THE POLISH JOINT DOWN THE END OF SANTA MONICA?
I CAN FIND IT.
I'LL BE THERE. TONIGHT. UNLESS YOU INSIST ON PIZZA...
FUNNY.
CLICK

That night.
Corner of Santa Monica and Lincoln Boulevards.
Think?
SZCZESNY
THANKS FOR COMING. HAVE A SEAT.
WASN'T SURE YOU'D SHOW, SO I GOT STARTED EARLY. BUT WE CAN GET YOU--
I'M NOT HUNGRY.
FAIR ENOUGH.
YOU KNOW, FIRST I HEARD OF YOU, WORD WAS THAT YOU DROVE, THAT'S ALL YOU DID.
TRUE AT THE TIME. THINGS CHANGED. SO DID I.
NO. WHAT YOU DID WAS ADAPT. GOT BY.
TIME YOU'RE TEN, TWELVE YEARS OLD, IT'S PRETTY MUCH SET IN YOU WHAT YOU'RE GOING TO BE LIKE.
AND YOU'VE BEEN ON A ROLL, BOY. CUT YOURSELF QUITE A SWATH OUT THERE.
I NEVER ASKED FOR ANY OF IT.
WE USUALLY DON'T. BUT IT COMES DOWN ON OUR HEADS REGARDLESS. HAPPENED THE SAME WITH NINO...
WE'D BEEN TOGETHER SINCE BEFORE I CAN REMEMBER. GREW UP TOGETHER IN BROOKLYN.
...I'M SORRY.
DON'T BE. HE'S HAD IT COMING AWHILE NOW.
SUCCESS OUT HERE WENT TO HIS HEAD. HE STARTED MAKING A LOT OF BAD DECISIONS. WENT A BIT TOO FAR...

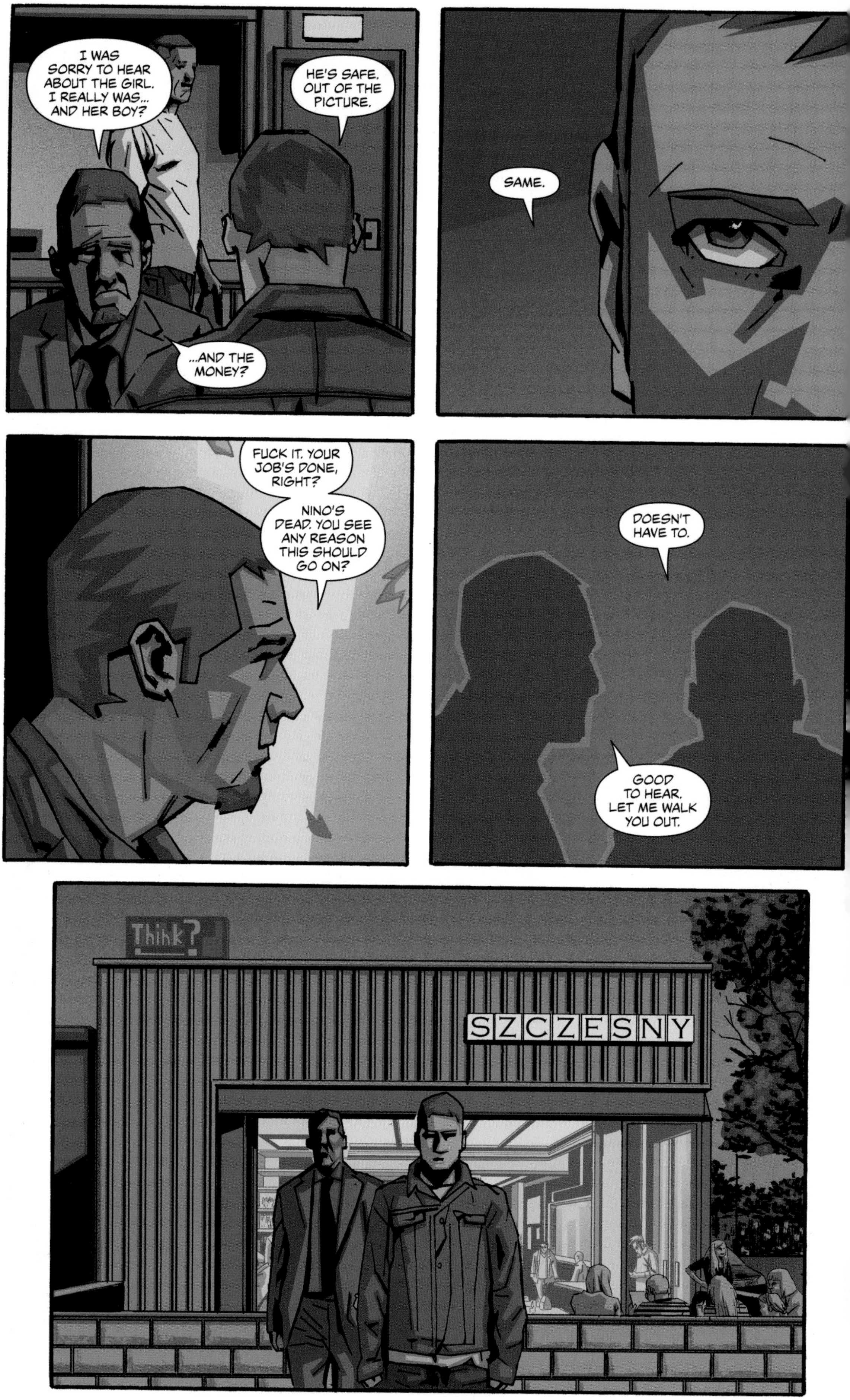
I WAS SORRY TO HEAR ABOUT THE GIRL. I REALLY WAS... AND HER BOY?
HE'S SAFE. OUT OF THE PICTURE.
...AND THE MONEY?
SAME.
FUCK IT. YOUR JOB'S DONE, RIGHT?
NINO'S DEAD. YOU SEE ANY REASON THIS SHOULD GO ON?
DOESN'T HAVE TO.
GOOD TO HEAR. LET ME WALK YOU OUT.
Think?
SZCZESNY

SO WHERE DO YOU GO FROM HERE?
HARD TO SAY. NOT BACK TO MY OLD LIFE. BURNED TOO MANY BRIDGES FOR THAT.
8
WELL, IT'S ABOUT TIME I MOVED ON. BACK EAST, I'M THINKING.
NEVER MUCH LIKED IT OUT HERE ANYWAY.
GUESS WE WON'T BE SEEING ONE ANOTHER AGAIN. TAKE CARE, BOY.

LISTEN...
...FOR SIRENS.
SCREECH OF TIRES.
A CALL FOR HELP.
NOTHING. JUST ANOTHER UGLY STREET STRETCHING ON THROUGH A CITY OF UGLY STREETS.
MAYBE HE'S RIGHT. MAYBE IT'S TIME I MOVED ON TO SOMETHING ELSE. AND MAYBE THAT'S IT...

SKREEEEE
...MAYBE ONE MORE BODY IS ENOUGH.

BY ANTONIO FUSO COLORS BY JASON LEWIS

THE

THURSDAY EDITION

ORGANIZED

It is no surprise to citizens of Los Angeles that crime is on the rise in their city. Reports released by the LAPD earlier this year showed a dramatic increase in robbery and aggravated assault, but L.A. residents need only look out their windows and onto their streets to see how bad things have actually gotten. Motor vehicle theft, muggings, and even murder are seen in every neighborhood, and behind each stolen car and chalk outline, there is another suspect that the already overburdened police force struggles to track down.

There are many who believe criminal activity could not have reached such a degree without the influence of several large-scale criminal organizations. Gangs and crime families are as much a part of L.A.'s history as the movie industry, and the LAPD is continually criticized for not doing enough to crack down on such groups. Until recently, the true identities of the individuals at the highest level of these organizations was a mystery to the public at large, but a recent string of robberies and murders has cast a spotlight on the fall of two of the city's more predominant gangsters.

"The murders of Isaiah Paolozzi and Bernard Rose are still under investigation," said LAPD

ISAIAH "NINO" PAOLOZZI

BERNAR

Detective Gil Franks during a press confere
"But we believe they are closely related to
eral recent deaths and that the two men wer
the head of a local criminal syndicate with
to the East Coast Mafia."

Both men were found dead yesterday, and s
clues beyond the two men's known associat
link their murders, according to police. Isai
"Nino" Paolozzi's body was discovered just
side his Brentwood home early in the morni
Paolozzi died of multiple gunshot wounds, a
cording to the L.A. County Coroner, and tw
were considered "contact gunshot wounds"

NGELS TIMES

E NEWS FROM THE CITY OF ANGELS

RIME TAKES A HIT IN L.A

left gunpowder residue on his skin, meaning the weapon was fired at close range.

Paolozzi's widow, who discovered the body and contacted the authorities shortly after, denies any knowledge of her late husband's criminal activity or connections to the Mafia, but police have asked her not to leave the country in case she is needed for further questioning.

Bernard Rose's body was discovered in a parking lot at the corner of Santa Monica and Lincoln Boulevards on the same evening of Paolozzi's death. Rose died from a stab wound to the neck, according to an account from the person who discovered the body, but police have released no further information about the circumstances surrounding what must have been a very public struggle to the death.

The other recent deaths Detective Franks referred to include a body that was pulled from Long Beach Harbor earlier this week, later identified as a known associate of Paolozzi who has an extensive criminal record and was suspected in a recent robbery and murder in the outskirts of Santa Monica. Another suspect in the robbery, who was identified from video surveillance footage, was later found dead at the scene of a violent mid-da shootout in a hotel room not far from the robber Two armed assailants were also killed, but law enforcement officials have released no information about the other individual who was involve and reportedly fled the scene shortly after.

There is an element that connects these crimes that police have not publicly revealed, but it is glaringly obvious to those who have followed these cases and can read between the lines. In many instances, a single individual—often described as a young, white male of average height and build—has been reported by eye-witnesses a fleeing the scene, racing away in a non-descript sedan that seems to slip from their collective memories as soon as it departs.

There are hundreds of crimes that go unsolved in Los Angles every year, but the one thing that con nects these in particular is quite possibly the person responsible for the deaths of Isaiah Paolozzi and Bernard Rose. These two men certainly did the citizens of L.A. no favors, so what can be sai of this mysterious figure who has toppled their criminal empire while narrowly evading the authorities? Is this a person closely connected to Paolozzi and Rose's organization, seeking to grasp the reigns of power for himself, or is he seeking some form of personal justice? And furthermore, is this the last we see of him, or is this simply where the trail of bodies begins?

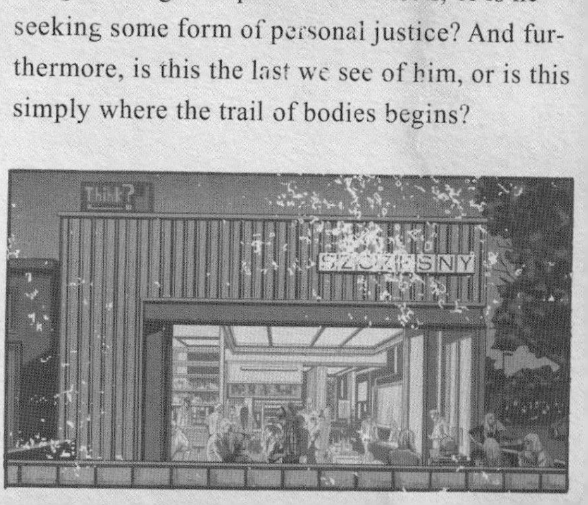

BY MIKE COLLINS

IDW FIRST EDITION MC515
#2 (of 4)
JAMES SALLIS'
DRIVE
THERE'S A LOT MORE MONEY HERE THAN THERE OUGHTA BE.
BY MICHAEL BENEDETTO AND ANTONIO FUSO

BY MIKE COLLINS

IDW
FIRST EDITION
MC615
#3 (of 4)
$3.99
JAMES SALLIS'
DRIVE
HE TOOK EVERYTHING THAT CAME HIS WAY...
AND WENT LOOKING FOR MORE.
POLICE LINE DO NOT CROSS POLICE LINE DO NOT CROSS POLICE L
BY MICHAEL BENEDETTO AND ANTONIO FUSO

BY MIKE COLLINS

IDW
FIRST EDITION
MC715
#4 (of 4)
JAMES SALLIS'
DRIVE
TRAVEL AGENT
CITY CENTER HARDWARE
WE'RE PROFESSIONALS. PEOPLE MAKE DEALS, THEY NEED TO STICK TO THEM.
BY MICHAEL BENEDETTO AND ANTONIO FUSO

BY MIKE COLLINS

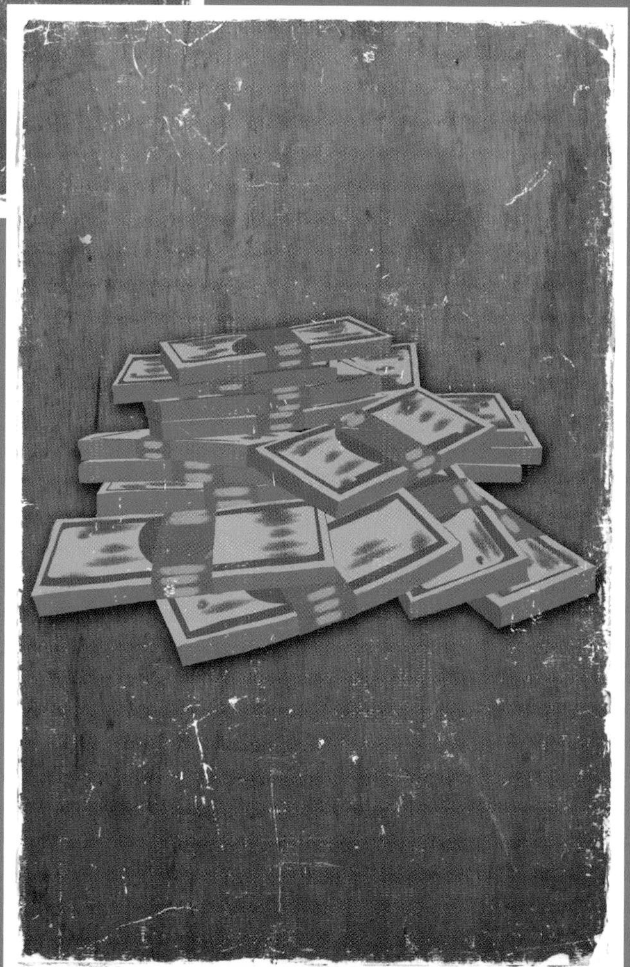

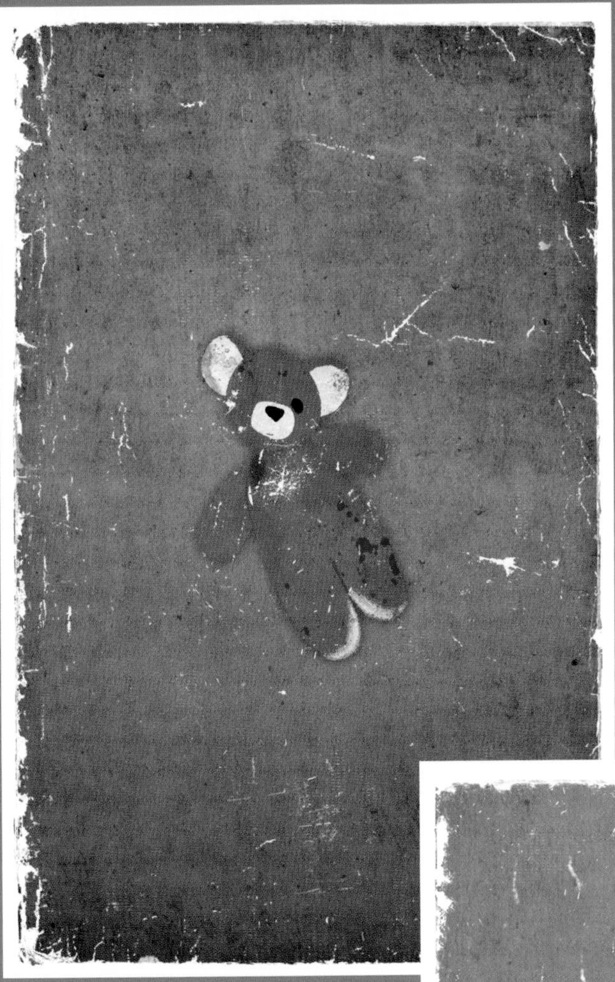

BY MIKE COLLINS

BY ADAM GORHAM COLORS BY MICHAEL SPICER

BY FRANCESCO FRANCAVILLA

JAMES SALLIS SPEAKS

THE ART OF TURNING *DRIVE* INTO A COMIC BOOK

There's so much about L.A. in Drive, *you must have a strong connection to the city. Have you ever lived in L.A.?*

I've not lived there, but for two years I taught in the MFA program at Otis College, commuting weekly. L.A. friends helped when I had specific questions.

How about industry stuff out this way. Have you ever worked in Hollywood or on a movie set?

My sole experience has been visiting the set as *Drive* was being filmed. It was as though an occupying army had taken over the region—dozens of trailers, tents, a huge kitchen and mess compound, soldiers scurrying about with equipment and walkie-talkies, nothing but film world in every direction.

Drive *obviously has a strong undercurrent of car culture—at least as it relates to the concept of freedom for young men. Do you consider yourself a car aficionado/gearhead?*

I can barely get a car started and back out of my driveway. The car stuff was researched. Luckily I have as friends both a professional test driver and a policeman with special training in automobiles and accident investigation.

With this story, there's an abundance of small details scattered throughout that lend a strong sense of authenticity. What kind of research did you do to prepare yourself for the book?

Most of it, frankly, comes from imagination. My way of writing is to fully visualize things in my own mind, then select what Chekhov called "specific, telling details."

Have you ever worked with or known a stuntman?

Again, research—books and the Internet.

There are a lot of movie references in Drive. *What kind of movies would you say most inspired this book?*

The movie references weren't a part of the original concept; they grew organically from the story itself. I have a driver, he works in Hollywood, he's involved with movies... But as I've noted before, films have had a major influence on everything I write. The way I write, the way I move stories along, is scenic, open, something I learned from decades of foreign, especially French, films. While science fiction movies of the Fifties, along with my reading of science fiction and fantasy, inculcated in me an assurance that the world is not as we see it—that other worlds co-exist around, beside, and behind our own.

What other authors/books most inspired this take on noir fiction?

The true origin of *Drive* lies in my wanting to write a contemporary equivalent of classic Gold Medal and other original-paperback novels from the Fifties. You bought them on wire racks in drug stores and bus stops. They were short, powerful, packed. They had weight, they moved.

What was the inspiration for the main character, Driver?

It all began, as most of my novels do, with a visual image: a man, injured, the sounds in the room, other bodies. I jotted that down on a legal pad—essentially the first scene as you read it now—and carried that page around with me for years before picking it out of the litter and beginning to ask the necessary questions. Who is this man? Why is he here? As I wrote, I came to realize I was writing, in effect, a contemporary Western: the mysterious, isolated stranger comes into town and, wishing only to be left alone, nonetheless is moved to put things right before riding out again. Into the sunset—that became quite explicit at book's end.

How did Bernie and Nino take shape as characters and as plot points?

Like Driver himself, they developed organically as I wrote. I've little idea what a book is or where it might go when I begin. I improvise—find my story as I write. If I'm surprised at what comes onto the page, I assume the reader will be as well.

You started out writing science fiction, right? How did you transition to crime and detective novels?

Changes in the science fiction landscape, changes in what I read, changes in what I was trying to do—in my reach. A lot of this I owe to Mike Moorcock, who introduced me to Hammett and Chandler while I was in London with him helping edit *New Worlds*.

Also I came onto a wealth of European literature I would never have encountered in the States—Cortazar, Queneau, Vian, French and Polish poetry. Upon return, I found Chester Himes and, reading forward to writers such as Stephen Greenleaf and Roger L. Simon, began to suspect that some of the best writing was being done in the mystery genre. Eventually I went around back and tried to slip in the back door.

So much in this novel works well in a visual medium. Did you have hopes that Drive *would have a life beyond the original novel when you wrote it?*

Rejected by New York publishers as too short and too idiosyncratic, it came close to having no life at all. My friend Rob Rosenwald at The Poisoned Pen felt differently and published it. My agent Steve Fisher in Hollywood would not give up on it; he was certain it would be a movie, and kept it moving in the waters. The novel sold, and sat for five years. But producer Marc Platt had the same faith that Rob and Steve had—and delivered the baby.

What was it like seeing your novel get the full-blown Hollywood treatment, and being prepped for the big screen?

As a man who lives on words, I hate to say indescribable, but it was. My wife and I attended the premiere in L.A. I always claim that I never moved the whole time. Except, Karyn reminds me, for the many times I flinched or pulled back in my seat. From the first shot, I was in Driver's world.

Now that we're moving along with the series, what were your initial thoughts when we approached you about comic books?

That the story, so visual and so concentrated, would translate wonderfully into graphic novels. I had little notion at the time, of course, how deeply respectful you are towards the novel—how the graphic novels would be a true re-creation.

Are you a fan of comic books? Did you ever read them as a kid?

Yes, right alongside Richard Matheson, Hemingway, Robert Heinlein, Theodore Sturgeon, John O'Hara, Edna St. Vincent Millay, John Steinbeck, *The Magazine of Fantasy & Science Fiction*, cereal boxes…

Can you tell us a little bit about what is in store for fans of the series in the sequel, Driven*?*

We know how Driver's story begins, and we know, from the last pages, how it will end. *Driven* fills in those years between where *Drive* ends and where Driver does.

Do you have any plans for further novels in the series?

No, but I didn't have any plan to write a sequel either, so…

What kind of car do you drive now?

A Hyundai sedan, a Nissan pickup. Both kind of limp along, as do I.

What's the craziest driving stunt you've ever pulled?

Staying alive the one time I tried driving in L.A.

Have you ever been in a high-speed chase?

Only between my intentions and what actually gets written.

ANTONIO FUSO Q&A

BRINGING *DRIVE* TO COMICS

Antonio, we're two issues in—what's it been like working on Drive*?*

Absolutely great, thanks!

For a story about something as motion-based as driving, did you have any reservations or concerns about porting that action onto the comics page?

When I read the first script I was a little bit worried thinking about all that car action to draw! I thought a lot about the right way to give a sense of speed to my art, and what I found was a combination of "kinetic lines" and handmade SFX. I hope readers will appreciate!

Before working on this project had you read the book or only seen the film? And what elements did you relate to?

Only seen the movie and I love it. I'd seen the movie three or four times even before knowing I had to draw the comic adaptation! Also the soundtrack is in my stereo right now while I'm working on issue 3!

Some of your highest profile gigs have been on noir-ish or espionage-themed material where there's a lot of quiet tension in a scene, and Drive *is no different. Do you seek out projects like that, or is that just how things go?*

I'm not the one searching for noir-ish stories... noir-ish stories are searching for me (and they get their target)! Well, to tell the truth my massive use of black ink makes me an easy choice if you want to put together a noir book! But in my dreams I would like to draw something with monsters and aliens in the future. :)

I know this is the first time any of you have worked together, so what has it been like collaborating with writer Michael Benedetto and colorist Jason Lewis?

Well, Michael is great and always really open when I propose some changes on the script (Michael, would you marry me :))! And Jason is incredible. He is not the kind of colorist who just does his "homework" if you know what I mean—coloring green trees, blue sky and yellow sun. He puts his own point of view and personality on pages and everything looks stunning and tastes of gun powder and bubble gum!

What's your favorite scene in the comic so far?

The first stunt sequence!

How about Driver's lofty morals and standards—that kinda attitude cut it in the world of professional comic book creators?

Professional comic book creators got no morals! Ahahaha

Anything else to add for readers as we round the corner and start heading for that parking lot in Santa Monica?

This is issue two and you are only halfway. The best is yet to come!

Well thanks for taking time to answer these questions... now get back to work on issue #3! ;-)

Oh, come on! :)

ANTONIO FUSO
SKETCHBOOK

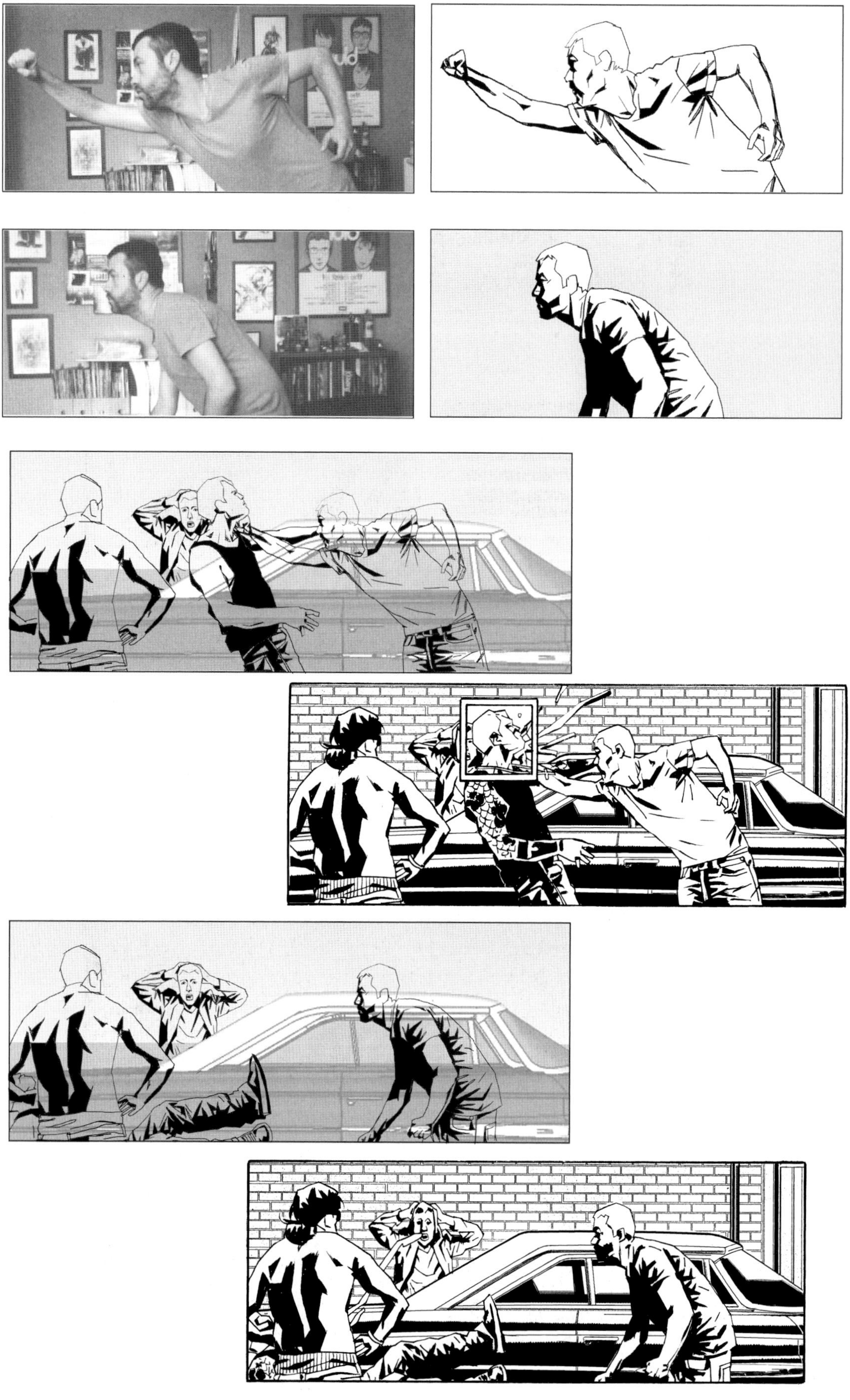

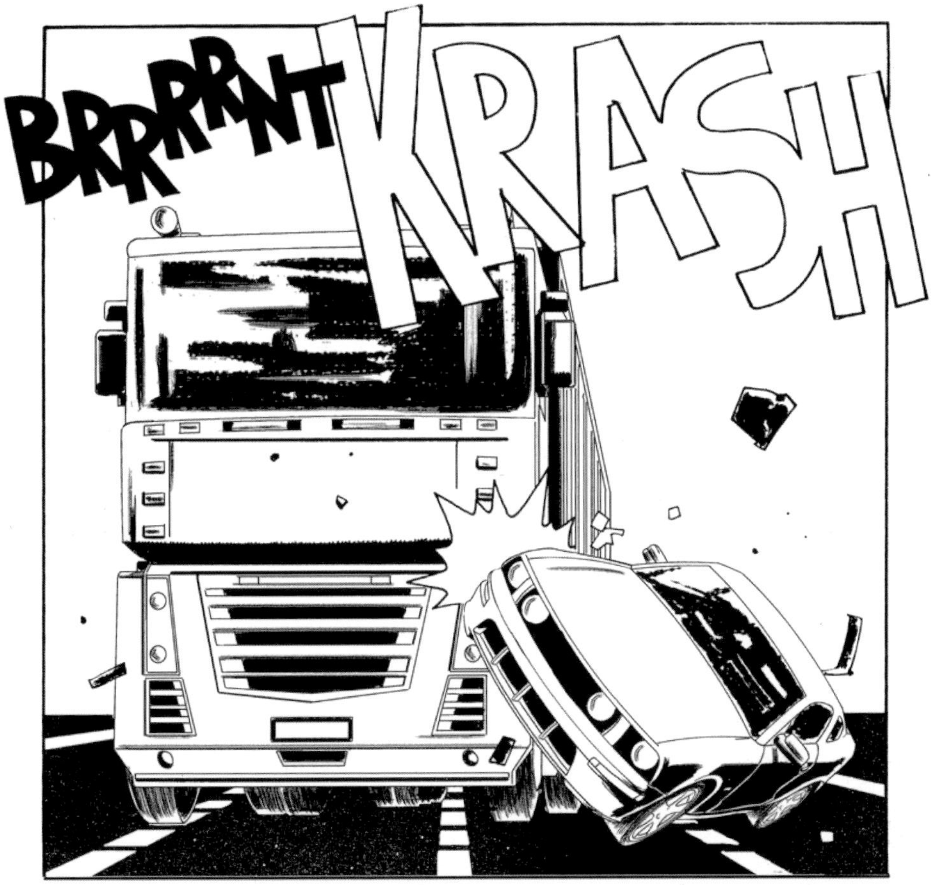
BRRRRRNT
KRASH

MICHAEL BENEDETTO Q&A

BRINGING *DRIVE* TO COMICS

Michael, we're three issues in—what's it been like working on Drive*?*

It's been unreal. I've read comics my whole life and have been lucky enough to have a hand in making them over the past couple years, but being so involved from square one and finally seeing the book in print is an amazing feeling.

Drive *is a story that many people know because of a movie, but the movie doesn't exactly line up with the story we're telling from the book. What's it been like trying to bridge that gap and adapt across mediums?*

A bit challenging but a lot of fun. The story we're telling is definitely different from the movie, but it's also different from James Sallis' novel. There are aspects of the story that work great for film and some that work better for prose. With the comic, we wanted to deliver a faithful retelling of the novel with a nod to the style of the movie, and I think we did really well striking the right balance.

Before working on this project had you read the book or only seen the film? And what elements did you relate to?

I had only seen the film and remain a huge fan. Despite the little we know about him and what little he says, Driver is such a strong character. Reading the book was a whole new experience since we get so much of Driver's backstory. Again, striking this balance in the comic was important to me. We still get the Driver who speaks more with his actions than words, but behind the poker face, we see how and why the gears are turning.

So, before Drive*, how many comic books had you written? Has this experience broadened your creative horizons in any way?*

Approximately zero—so, yes. Horizons broadened! I've done a lot of writing and even some collaborating with other artists but never for a visual medium like this and never to this scale. Seeing the first comic I ever wrote in print—there's nothing like it. And I hope it's the first of many!

I know this is the first time any of you have worked together, so what has it been like collaborating with artist Antonio Fuso and colorist Jason Lewis?

A real pleasure and a great learning experience. Being teamed up with these guys—who are both incredibly talented artists—is more than I could possibly have hoped for in a first book. Antonio's hyper-realistic landscapes and classic cars always amaze me, and Jason's colors are always jaw dropping and have really taken this book to the next level. This being my first professional comic collaboration, I've learned so much from working with them. Many, many thanks to you both!

What's your favorite scene in the comic so far?

I love the final showdown with Cook in this issue. I'm really happy with how that turned out, and it's good to see Cook finally get what's coming to him. But the best stuff is still coming up next issue in my opinion, so stay tuned!

How about Driver's lofty morals and standards—that kinda attitude cut it in the world of professional comic book creators?

I don't think I could ever match Driver's intensity or his convictions, and if I did, they might get me stuffed in a trunk. But in all seriousness, all the people I work with in the comic book world are awesome, hard-working people, and everyone is ready to do whatever needs doing to see the job done. Even though Driver wouldn't admit it at first, he's the same way.

Anything else to add for readers as we round the corner and start heading for that parking lot in Santa Monica?

Just to thank everyone for reading and to get ready for the high-speed, revenge-fueled conclusion next issue... and for what we've got coming up on the horizon...

Well thanks for taking time to answer these questions... we've got the art team working on #4 so I guess you and I will just have to keep concentrating on DRIVEN*!*

Yes, *DRIVEN*! I just finished reading the book, and I'm very excited to buckle in for another road trip with everyone's favorite man behind the wheel. Lots of crazy twists and turns up ahead—we'll have to see if Driver can pull it off. See you all there!

JASON LEWIS Q&A

BRINGING *DRIVE* TO COMICS

Jason, we're at the finish line—what's it been like working on Drive*?*

It's been an absolute blast! It's rare that the "perfect" project comes along that'll let you go all out and really showcase what you can do.

Drive *is a story that many people know because of a movie, but the movie doesn't exactly line up with the story we're telling from the book. What's it been like trying to bridge that gap and adapt across mediums?*

Antonio and Michael did the real heavy lifting there, so my job was easy by comparison. When I signed on my editor told me to think of it like I'm adapting the soundtrack from the film, which gave me the license to go totally impressionistic and crazy with the colors. I tried to use my palettes to dig at the emotional core of the panels rather than replicate anything I'd previously seen on screen.

Before working on this project had you read the book or only seen the film? And what elements did you relate to?

I hadn't read the book, but I was very familiar with the film. One of the first dates I went on with my ex-girlfriend was to see *Drive* in the theaters. Even though that relationship ran out of gas I still have fond memories of seeing the movie.

Being a freelance artist I could really relate to the sense of isolation and detachment you get from the Driver character. Except in my case, instead of being a murder machine or a whiz with cars, I'm really good at coloring comic books.

So, before Drive*, how many comic books had you colored? Has this experience broadened your creative horizons in any way?*

I had been coloring comics professionally for several years, but the majority of my mainstream output had been all-ages books. Work is work, but I had become pigeonholed in the industry as someone who could only color kid's comics, and thus was getting passed over for superhero, horror and other more adult genres. *Drive* changed all that and now I'm getting a far wider range of projects offered to me. These days editors are more afraid that I'll drown all my pages in magenta and nuclear green or give everyone neon skin tones, which is progress.

I know this is the first time any of you have worked together, so what has it been like collaborating with artist Antonio Fuso and writer Michael Benedetto?

Even though I'd seen the movie a bunch of times, Michael's writing constantly caught me off guard and wondering what was going to happen next. That's no easy feat for someone adapting well known source material. Kudos to you Michael! You pulled it off beautifully!

I'd been a fan of Antonio's work since his early *Cobra* stuff. Even though his art is very angular and stylized it's grounded in a solid, gritty realism which anchors all my insane coloring. Together I feel we pulled off one of the cooler looking books that I've seen on the racks in recent memory.

What's your favorite scene in the comic so far?

I like all the scenes where Driver is interacting with someone one-on-one. Usually those are the boring parts of a comic, but here they gave me an opportunity to get creative with the colors to better enhance the mood of the conversations being depicted.

How about Driver's lofty morals and standards—that kinda attitude cut it in the world of professional comic book creators?

You have to be kind of a mercenary to sustain any freelance career. Much like Driver, I'm really good at this one thing. If you hire me and give me the freedom to do what I do you won't be disappointed with the results. I wish I could think of a more baddass way of adapting Driver's business speech to coloring comics.

Anything else to add for readers as we round the corner and start heading for that parking lot in Santa Monica?

I'm really appreciative of all the fan support *Drive* has received. I'm constantly getting hit up on Twitter or approached at conventions by folks super stoked on *Drive's* colors. Stay tuned people, the cool stuff is just beginning!

Well thanks for taking time to answer these questions... maybe we'll all get to play in this sandbox again for DRIVEN*!*

No one is looking forward to *Driven* more than me. Can't wait to see everyone there!

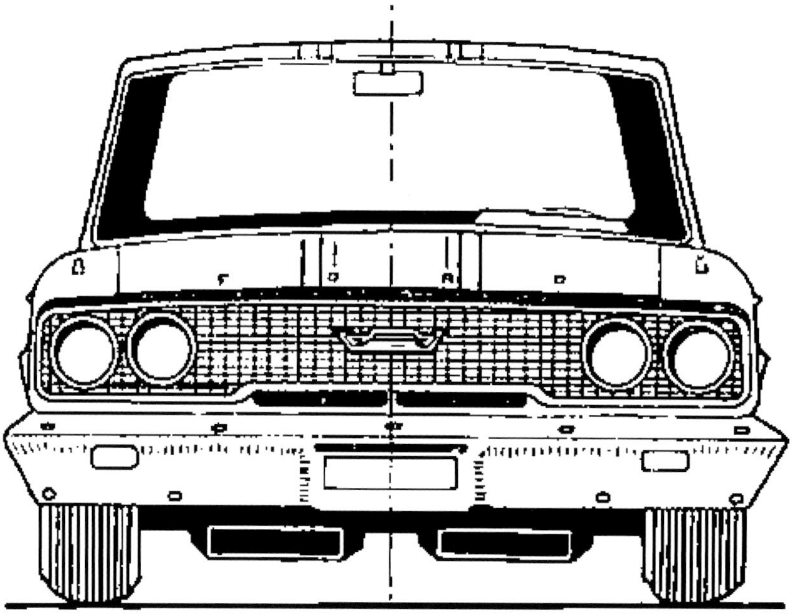

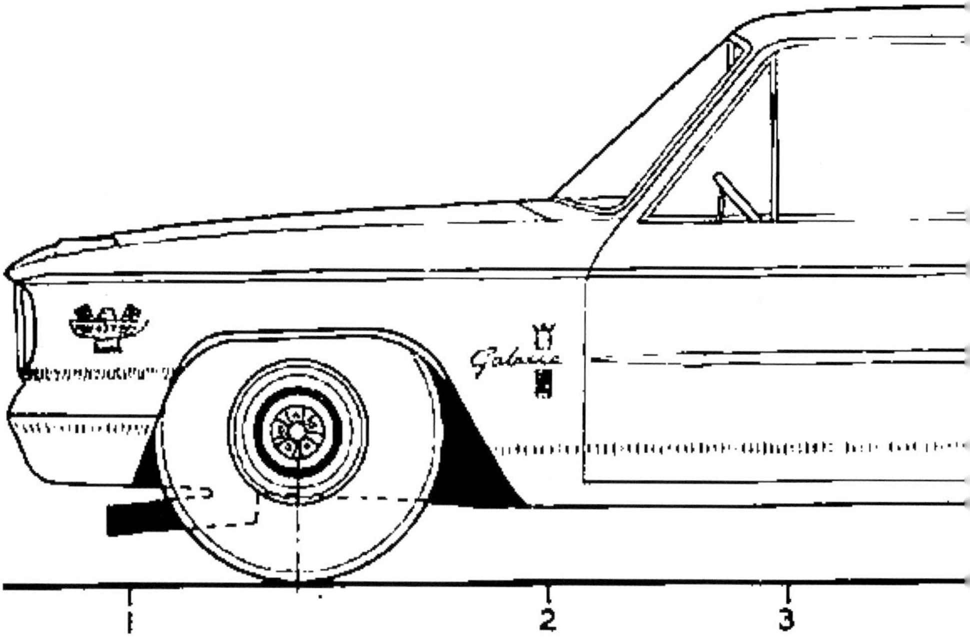
1
2
3

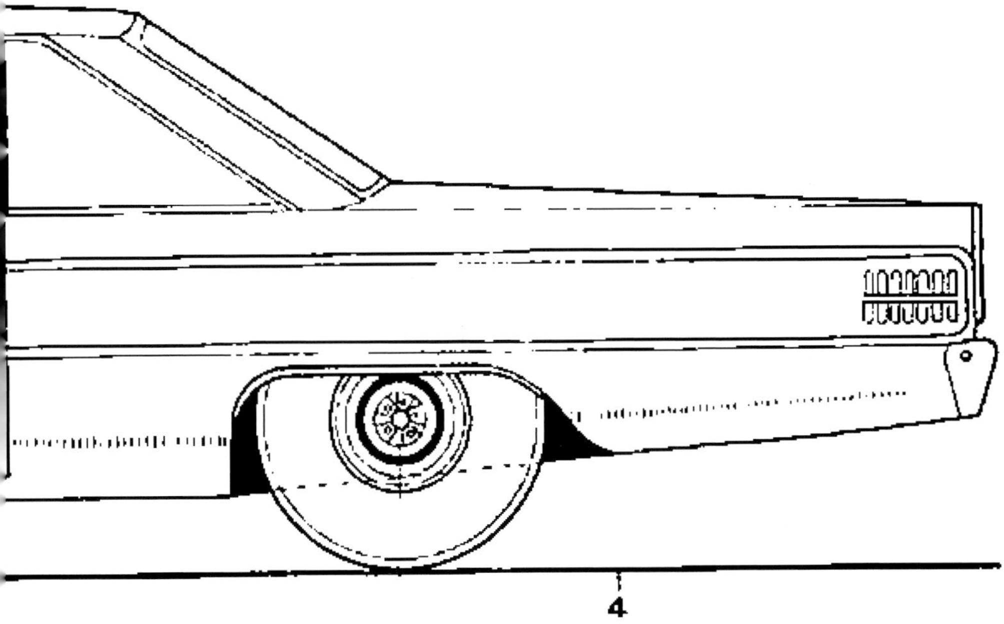
4

TIPS FROM A DRIVER

"Stunt Driving" should be performed only by a trained professional under ideal and controlled circumstances.

However, that doesn't mean we can't ask a working stunt driver how some of the most popular moves are done.

PART 1

As we see in the story, Driver executes a turn at high speed, spins 180° to maintain speed in reverse, and then swings around forward to race down an alley. Very cool. But not so easy. There's actually several steps involved, one of which is the stunt driving basic known simply as "a drift." So we'll start with that. Here are three ways to try it with a rear-wheel-drive car...

IF YOUR VEHICLE HAS DECENT HORSEPOWER...

TECHNIQUE #1: POWER-OVER

1) Turn the wheel back and forth quickly to gain control of the way the weight is distributed.

2) Now lay on the throttle, heavy at first, followed by more controlled feathering.

3) At the same time, counter steer (the steering wheel) as the car breaks into the slide. At this point you're relying solely on momentum.

4) Hit your mark, and take off to wherever you've gotta go.

ANOTHER WAY OF DOING THIS IS PRETTY SIMILAR AND PREFERABLE FOR CARS WITH LESS POWER...

TECHNIQUE #2: KICK IT

1) Turn the steering wheel back and forth to transfer weight and gain control of the weight distribution.

2) With your foot on the throttle, depress the clutch pedal and quickly release. (Clutch Kick.)

3) Simultaneously counter steer with the steering wheel and the back end will come out.

4) Regulate the throttle (off and on/feathering it), steering with the momentum and continuing to counter steer until you've successfully made it through the corner.

5) Slowly let off the gas to straighten out and bring the steering wheel back to center.

LOOKING FOR SOMETHING MORE DRAMATIC? TRY THIS ONE...

TECHNIQUE #3: THE E-BRAKE

1) At full speed, lightly transfer the weight back and forth with the steering wheel to gain control of the weight distribution.

2) While turning the wheel in the direction you want the car to turn, depress the clutch pedal, let off the throttle, and yank on the e-brake.

3) As the rear end slides out, let off the clutch and slam on the gas.

YOU JUST DROVE LIKE A BADASS!

Melissa Miller is a San Diego-based stunt driver and drift racer. When not rebuilding her custom Nissan, she can be seen sliding through the turns at Extreme AutoFest and Hot Import Nights, or find her on the Speed channel's drift show "Whipped." www.MelissaDrifts.com

BY ADAM GORHAM COLORS BY MICHAEL SPICER

BY VASSILIS GOGTZILAS

TIPS FROM A DRIVER

"Stunt Driving" should be performed only by a trained professional under ideal and controlled circumstances.

However, that doesn't mean we can't ask a working stunt driver how some of the most popular moves are done.

PART 2

In this issue of Drive, *there's a scene on a film set where Driver must perform a maneuver that puts the stunt car up on two wheels. In stunt driving parlance, this is often referred to as "skiing" or "high skiing." It seems very risky and difficult, though a quick YouTube search will show countless videos from Saudi Arabia of people performing these stunts on the open road, with cars full of friends, actually getting out of the car and even changing a tire mid-stunt!*

To find out everything we could about driving on two wheels and whether or not it is possible to do on a stock automobile, professional driver Terry Grant walked us through the trick...

IN ORDER TO DO A PROPER TWO WHEEL STUNT...

THE BASICS

1) Inflate the tires that will remain on the ground to 80psi.

2) Set up a 10ft-long ramp that's about 30 inches tall.

3) Drive the tires with regular tire pressure onto the ramp at a speed of about 30 mph (though speed can vary by vehicle).

4) As the car pops onto two wheels quickly turn the steering wheel towards the high side.

5) With the car's weight wanting to roll onto the roof, catch the balance with another quick flick of the steering wheel.

6) Maintain balance by constantly making side-to-side adjustments with the steering wheel.

7) End your stunt by turning the wheel towards the high-side, forcing the car back onto four wheels.

ARE YOU DRIVING ON THE HIGH-SIDE OR THE LOW-SIDE...

VARIATIONS

1) Though it's most common to perform the stunt while driving on the low-side, it can be done either way.

2) If planning a high-side two-wheel stunt, stronger tires are suggested that feature much larger sidewalls to allow enough surface area for balance.

3) In addition to different tires, high-side stunt driving cars are usually outfitted with more gear for bracing and support.

4) Low-side driving is generally preferred because it allows for faster driving and longer distances.

SURPRISE, YOU'RE DRIVING ON TWO WHEELS...

COMMON MISTAKES

1) The most common mistake is missing the initial "catch" and rolling the car onto the roof. Try to avoid this.

2) Letting off the gas as the car leaves the ramp. Terry explains that the forward motion of acceleration contributes to the car's balance, making the stunt possible.

3) Prolonged two-wheel driving WILL destroy the front tire from strain and pressure.

YOU JUST DROVE LIKE A BADASS!

Terry Grant is a UK-based stunt driver with 21 World Records to his name. He has performed at such prestigious events as the Race of Champions in Paris, the World Rallycross in Argentina, the London Motorshow, and the TV studios of Guiness World Records in Madrid, while working with such manufacturers as General Motors, Saab, Nissan, and TVR. His current sponsors include Monster Energy and Power Maxed. Find out where and when to see him work his magic at www.TerryGrant.com.

TIPS FROM A DRIVER

"Stunt Driving" should be performed only by a trained professional under ideal and controlled circumstances.

However, that doesn't mean we can't ask a working stunt driver how some of the most popular moves are done.

PART 3

By issue #3 of Drive*, stakes have risen and the threat of harm is greatly increased. Driver himself has been stitched up and members of his crew have been less fortunate. But now, with a plan of action on how to extract himself from this predicament, Driver must elude his pursuers and stay a few steps ahead. In order to do that, he's going to employ some basic (and not so basic) tricks to detecting and shaking a tail.*

And to make sure all our info was legit we reached out to an expert—but this time our professional doesn't want any credit, listing or notoriety. So here's what we learned about evading a tail and getting out of Dodge.

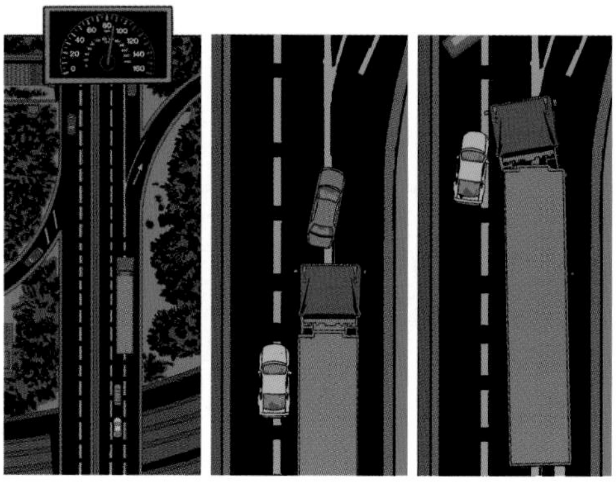

KNOWING WHEN IT'S TIME TO GET LOST...

SPOTTING A TAIL

1) Recognizing surveillance starts with being aware of your surroundings. Pay attention to the people and vehicles within your vicinity. Don't ignore a gut feeling.

2) Most of today's pros employ a multi-car tail, but low-level criminals don't have those resources so they're most likely to use one vehicle. The good news is that this is the easiest to spot.

3) If a tail is following you, try speeding up and slowing down to be sure they are in fact on your tail.

4) If you are being tailed, continue to act natural. That leads us to...

WHEN FIGHT OR FLIGHT MEANS... RUN!

FIVE WAYS TO LOSE A TAIL

1) Run a red light or drive the wrong way on a one-way street to further identify a tail vehicle.

2) While traveling at high speed on a freeway, quickly cut across four lanes of traffic and exit.

3) After rounding a blind curve, make a bootlegger's turn (See Issue #1) and take off in the opposite direction.

4) Turn a corner then pull over and park, noting all passing vehicles. Flush out your tail.

5) Use a semi-truck to block your move and drive the tailing car off the road.*

YOU JUST DROVE LIKE A BADASS!
**As seen in this issue.*

This issue's TIPS FROM A PRO was answered by a former professional stunt and getaway driver currently serving time in California for his role in an armed robbery. Stay out of jail, kids.

BY NELSON DÁNIEL

BY MATT LESNIEWSKI

TIPS FROM A DRIVER

"Stunt Driving" should be performed only by a trained professional under ideal and controlled circumstances.

However, that doesn't mean we can't ask a working stunt driver how some of the most popular moves are done.

PART 4

The end is nigh. Driver has his quarry in sight and the time of reckoning is upon us. But endings aren't always clean—this one is no different. It's a showdown between two capable killers, with little room for error. And when the margin of error is the soft, fleshy skin covering your own guts, well, maybe you should be prepared in case things don't go quite as planned.

That's how we leave Driver—bleeding out onto his interior as he speeds off into the night. Does he live? What's next? A lot of that has to do with just how much Driver knows about tending to a fresh wound.

But for the rest of us, here's some tips on how to pull yourself through a meeting with Bernie Rose.

SO YOU'VE SPRUNG A LEAK...

I'M STABBED: THE IMMEDIATE AFTERMATH

1) A sharp object has pierced your person and now a gory, possibly deadly leak needs attention.

2) A normal person would call 9-1-1. You are not a normal person doing legal things, so this is impossible.

3) Inspect the injury. How bad is it? This will determine how much effort to put into the following steps.
Note: A deeper wound has a higher chance of injuring an internal organ, which makes death much more likely.

APPLY PRESSURE AND PRAY...

THE CLOCK IS TICKING

4) Stop the bleeding. In Driver's case he's hurt, bad, but not bad enough to put him in the ground. So it's time to apply pressure to slow the bleeding.

5) Dress the wound. We see this in movies all the time, but it's true. Tie a tourniquet, keep applying pressure, and move on to...

6) Seek alternative medical care. You've got the bleeding under control, and seem to be stabilizing—but that hole isn't going to fix itself. Find someone handy with know-how that can get you patched up.
Or, you know, go to the hospital.

CONGRATS, YOU JUST SURVIVED LIKE A BADASS!

This issue's TIPS FROM A PRO was answered by a Southern California EMS professional. Stay safe out there. And apply pressure!

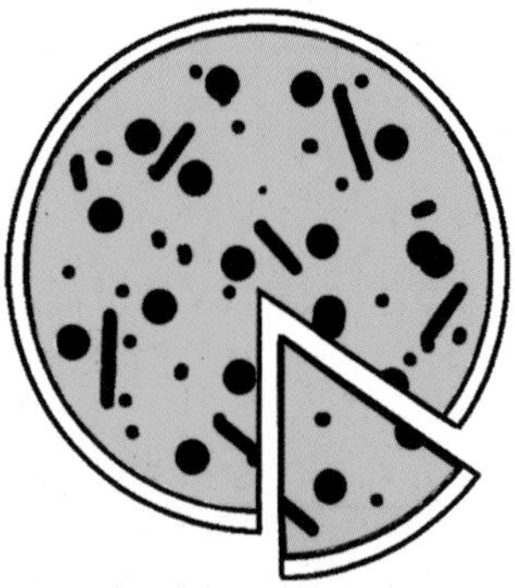

Nino's Pizza

FREE DELIVERY
WITH A MINIMUM PURCHASE OF $20

ORDER NOW
800-555-PIZZA